The Fighting Douglas MacArthur

Books by Clarke Newlon

1001 Questions Answered about Space

Famous Pioneers in Space

L.B.J., The Man from Johnson City

The Fighting Douglas MacArthur

The Fighting
Douglas MacArthur

by Clarke Newlon

ILLUSTRATED WITH PHOTOGRAPHS

AND MAPS

DODD, MEAD & COMPANY

NEW YORK

Second Printing

Printed in the United States of America
by The Cornwall Press, Inc., Cornwall, N. Y.

ILLUSTRATIONS

* *U.S. Army Photographs*

v

MacArthur signs the Japanese surrender document aboard the USS *Missouri*, August 31, 1945. Behind him are Generals Wainwright and Percival.

With Admiral Halsey and General Eichelberger, General MacArthur salutes the first American flag raised over the American Embassy in Tokyo since Pearl Harbor.

General MacArthur receives Emperor Hirohito in Tokyo.

Admiral Lord Louis Mountbatten, Supreme Allied Commander, Southeast Asia Theater, visits General MacArthur in Manila.

MacArthur's famous C-54, the *Bataan*.

General MacArthur with Mrs. MacArthur at the Manila independence ceremonies.

MacArthur with President Syngman Rhee at South Korean independence ceremonies, August 15, 1948.

General MacArthur speaks before the San Francisco City Hall after a half million Americans had welcomed him back to his home shores.

The General Douglas MacArthur Memorial Building in Norfolk, Virginia.

MacArthur statue at Inchon, Korea, where he made the landing which saved the nation and an American Army.

Douglas MacArthur makes his famous address to a joint session of Congress on April 19, 1951.

MAPS

The Fighting Douglas MacArthur

1

☆ ☆ ☆ ☆ ☆

Dusk was settling over Manila Bay when the PT boat slipped up to the war-ravaged dock at Corregidor as quietly as its three 4,000-horsepower motors would permit. There was no moon and, in the growing darkness, no sign of the patrolling Japanese warships that ringed the Philippine Islands of Luzon and Corregidor.

General Douglas MacArthur, exercising a commander's privilege to board last, stepped on the deck. He stood for a moment facing the tiny, rocky island where he had directed the magnificent defense of the Philippines for many weeks, then gave a quick order and turned away.

Naval Lieutenant John D. Bulkeley guided the craft from the mooring into the deeper darkness of Manila Bay and headed for the rendezvous point. There they met the other three boats of a tiny flotilla, loaded earlier at Sisiman Bay, on the Bataan coast.

It was March 11, 1942, about seven o'clock in the evening. Three months earlier, on December 7, 1941, the Japanese had bombed Pearl Harbor at Hawaii.

Thus began the most famous escape through enemy lines in history, the 2500-mile dash Douglas MacArthur made from

Corregidor to Australia, through hostile forces which controlled the sea and air—and most of the land—every foot of the way, taking with him eighteen members of his staff, his wife, his son and his son's nurse.

His report of the exploit to Army Headquarters in Washington was short and cryptically unadorned, but complete. It read:

Departed from Corregidor at dark with party of twenty-two [giving names], travelling on four United States Navy torpedo boats. Afternoon air reconnaissance revealed one hostile cruiser and one destroyer off west coast of Mindoro, but we slipped by them in the darkness. Passed following day in shelter of uninhabited island but risked discovery by air and started several hours before dark in order to approach Mindanao at dawn. Sighted enemy destroyer at 15,000 yards but escaped unseen, making scheduled run despite heavy seas and severe buffeting. Upon arrival Mindanao learned that of four planes dispatched only one had arrived and that, without brakes or supercharger and being unfit for mission, had already departed. [General] Brett selected three more planes for trip, of which one developed mechanical trouble and two arrived safely, taking entire party out. Safe arrival and departure forced us to pass latitude at Ambon at dawn but course set somewhat to eastward enabled party to escape interception. Landed Batchelor Field while Darwin under raid.

Behind the bare bones of this official statement is the dramatic story of the escape: the mine fields, the tense moments under the guns of enemy ships, the menace of Japanese aircraft and the ever-present misery and danger as the tiny PT boats fought the natural enmity of mountainous seas with faltering motors.

As Lieutenant Bulkeley * guided PT boat No. 41 around the mine fields to the rendezvous with the other three craft, he mentally checked off his passengers:

Aboard No. 41 were General MacArthur, his wife Jean MacArthur and son Arthur MacArthur (aged four years), Ah Cheu, the boy's Filipino *amah* or nurse, and military staff members: Major General Richard K. Sutherland, Chief of Staff; Naval Captain Herbert James Ray; Lieutenant Colonel Joseph Sherr and Lieutenant Colonel Sid Huff, General Mac-Arthur's aide-de-camp.

The four torpedo boats met at Turning Buoy, the prescribed point. They were: PTs 32, 34 and 35, in addition to No. 41. Aboard them were other members of MacArthur's staff, including: Brigadier Generals Richard Marshall, Spencer Akin, William Marquat, Hugh Casey and Harold George; Rear Admiral Francis W. Rockwell; Colonels Charles Willoughby and Paul Stivers; Lieutenant Colonels L. A. Diller and Francis Wilson; Major Charles H. Morhouse and Captain Joseph McMicking.

Roaring out into the open seas in diamond formation, with No. 41 leading, they saw the white flares from the patrolling Japanese craft, the customary alert signal, but apparently the noise of the PT boat motors was mistaken for aircraft overhead; they were not sighted.

The plan of escape on the first leg of the dash which would take General MacArthur to his new post in Australia as commander in chief of the United States Armed Forces, Far East, was uncomplicated. They were to cruise through the night

* This is the same John D. Bulkeley, now a Rear Admiral, who in February, 1964, cut the water lines to Guantanamo Naval Base after Castro's Cuban government had shut off the flow. Accused by Castro of taking water surreptitiously through the line, President Johnson ordered it cut so there could be no doubt. The United States supplied water to the base by tanker and then built a plant to remove salt from sea water.

and arrive at dawn at their destination, a small uninhabited island. There they would take cover during the day and proceed the following night to Mindanao, the southernmost of the Philippine Islands. From there, aircraft would fly them to Australia.

But it was not to be that simple. Out of the mouth of Manila Bay and passing the tiny Apo Islands, spray wet the magnetos of No. 41, forcing Bulkeley to stop and dry them off. All of the torpedo boats had seen arduous service. Their engines needed overhauls and repairs which had been impossible to accomplish due to war conditions in the Philippines. As the run continued, all four boats had engine trouble. They became separated, the formation was abandoned and each craft headed forward alone.

The PT boat of World War II was seventy-seven feet long and built of plywood, with mahogany hull. It was crewed by seventeen men. Its three Packard 4,000-horsepower motors drove triple screws which thrust the boat along at a top speed of forty knots an hour. The engines produced a vibration which shook the craft from stem to stern, and the power of the 12,000 total horses, tremendous for such a small craft, hurled the pounding hull forward with brute force. The PT boat was a roughrider in a calm harbor. In turbulent seas the action was murderous, a combination of bucking bronco and wallowing tub.

The South China Sea was far from calm as the four PTs made their dash out of Manila Bay this night of March 11, 1942. Young Arthur, with a stuffed rabbit, his only toy these days, and Ah Cheu, were placed in the officers' bunks. General MacArthur, Mrs. MacArthur and Colonel Huff sat on a mattress on the floor of the cockpit. The others sat or lay where they could find space and—with few exceptions—

succumbed to violent seasickness. General MacArthur himself said, "It was a bad night for everyone."

One of the narrowest escapes for the General came, ironically, from one of his own flotilla. During the first night, the PTs had become widely separated. Dawn—about 7 A.M.— found No. 41 cruising an empty sea. There was no sign of the three other craft, no sign of the rendezvous island, no sign of anything. It was a situation the Japanese would have forgone a major victory to have known about: here was the hero of Bataan, one of America's greatest generals, the commander of our Far East Armed Forces—alone and virtually unprotected in waters the Japanese dominated completely.

Like PT 41, the skipper of PT 32 had found himself far from his destination at dawn, but near the islands of the Cuyo group, some two hundred miles south of Manila Bay. As he headed for their protection, the lookout reported another ship on the near horizon. It looked, he declared, like a Japanese destroyer and was coming up fast.

PT 32 tried to run for cover, but its shaky engines fell short. The other ship continued to gain. The PT captain then ordered that the big extra fuel drums lashed to the deck be scuttled, clearing the deck for machine gun action. He manned and loaded two of the torpedo tubes.

Also aboard PT 32 were Brigadier Generals Akin and Casey, who sought out the captain and talked him into delaying hostile action. No one, they argued, had really had a good look at the approaching craft. It might be friendly.

The captain agreed and, at the end of many tense moments, one pair of binoculars brought into focus the easily recognizable silhouette of Douglas MacArthur, standing in the bow of the approaching boat—PT 41. Bulkeley was also seeking shelter for his valuable cargo from the naked exposure of the open sea.

Although they had escaped this momentary danger, the situation for the party was far from happy. They were still an hour or more from their destination, the island of Tagauayan. They were in danger of being spotted by enemy aircraft. They were separated from the other two PTs and there was, General MacArthur feared, the possibility of jeopardizing the entire escape expedition.

As they awaited a decision, the exhausted passengers dried themselves out. A pancake breakfast was served on deck. Arthur played with the cook's monkey, who went by the name of General Tojo. Precious gasoline was transferred from PT 41 to PT 32, which had jettisoned its drums. No one was allowed on the deserted shore except a lookout. He watched there with the full knowledge that, should the party be spotted, both PTs would make a run for it and he would be abandoned.

They were not spotted, but after several hours and several conferences with Bulkeley, who was willing to chance it, General MacArthur gave the order and the two PTs took off in full daylight for the meeting point at Tagauayan Island, some forty miles farther along the southward route to Mindanao. They had thought the seas might be calmer. They were not, and for something over an hour the MacArthurs and other passengers, soaked to the skin by the spray, suffered again the misery of buffeting waves and seasickness.

When the two craft made it to Tagauayan, they found PT 34 already there, having arrived at about nine-thirty that morning. There was no sign of the fourth boat, and the passengers of the three craft sweltered in the heat, hidden and camouflaged as well as possible under the circumstances, until six o'clock that evening.

Their time schedule would not permit further delay. PT 32, by this time, was operating on one engine and was, of course, out of fuel. Its passengers were divided between the other two boats and PT 32 and its crew were left behind. They were to await the arrival of a submarine, the *Permit*, which was due to arrive the next morning to check on the progress of MacArthur's dash through the lines.

(*Permit* arrived as scheduled and took the crew aboard. Before leaving Tagauayan, they blew up PT 32 to prevent its falling into enemy hands.)

The weather, which had been overcast, began worsening as the second stage of the journey got underway shortly after six. It was a blessing in that it helped the two PTs escape detection, but it added to the misery of those aboard. This time, PT 34 led and No. 41 followed in its wake. Although this maneuver helped those on the second craft, they were far from comfortable.

There were two brushes with the enemy that night. When the Americans were only a little more than an hour on their way, Lieutenant R. G. Kelly, in the lead craft, sighted a Japanese cruiser. It loomed huge in the gathering darkness, with armament which could easily have blown the PTs out of the water.

It was the sighting of this cruiser at fifteen thousand yards (about eight miles) that General MacArthur mentioned in his official report.

Lieutenant Kelly turned PT 34 sharp right rudder and Bulkeley, in No. 41, did the same. There followed some fifteen minutes of tense waiting, but the fugitives were never sighted . . . and then the sun went down.

A little later, as they were passing a Japanese-held island base, the roar of the PT engines alerted the shore defenses. Again, they were mistaken for aerial bombers, and from the PT boats the anxious watchers saw the searchlights scouring the sky in futile search.

The rest of the trip passed without incident, except for increasingly bad weather and rougher water as they went into the Sea of Mindanao. General MacArthur later described his recollections of the night as "like taking a trip in a concrete mixer."

The MacArthur party arrived at their destination, Cagayan, on the northern coast of Mindanao, about 9:00 A.M. Friday, March 13, relieved to find it still in American hands. They were equally relieved a little later when the missing PT boat, No. 35, arrived safely. General MacArthur was met by the commander of the forces on the island, Brigadier General William F. Sharp, from whom they learned several pieces of news.

First, General Sharp's troops were in control of the port and the nearby areas, but he said he did not know how much longer they could contain a determined enemy advance. Del Monte Airfield, where the bombers would land prior to taking the MacArthur party to Australia, was about twenty miles from the front lines and subject to intermittent air attack.

Second, due to a mixup in communications, three B-17 bombers which were to take the MacArthur party to Australia had taken off on March 12, one day early. One had developed engine trouble and turned back; a second, also with engine trouble, had crashed at sea, killing the pilot and co-pilot; the third had made it through on three good engines, but (along with brake and supercharge trouble) could not wait on the vulnerable airfield and had returned to its Australian base.

General MacArthur immediately ordered three more B-17s. Two arrived late in the evening of March 16, the third having turned back with the engine trouble which MacArthur, by this time, was beginning to believe was chronic. It was, he would learn later, due to the lack of spare parts for the few

American planes in that theater of war and to the scarcity of maintenance crews.

Each passenger on the escape from Corregidor had been allowed one suitcase for personal clothing. Now, with only two aircraft to fly the entire party out of Mindanao, orders were given that even these must be abandoned. Mrs. MacArthur later lost her handbag and arrived in Australia with a lipstick and comb tied up in a handkerchief.

The destination was Darwin, a seven-hour flight across the Pacific and the Japanese-held East Indies to the northeast tip of Australia. The latter was under Japanese air attack when the two B-17s approached early on the morning of March 17, so they diverted to Batchelor Field, forty miles away, a strip which had been graded out of the sand and brush of the desolate countryside. Darwin itself at that time was a seaport town of a few thousand people and near to nothing else civilized. It was, and still is, a government-built naval base.

Coming on top of the buffeting she had received at the hands of the PT boats, the rugged all-night trip in the bomber was almost too much for Jean MacArthur. There were no seats, of course, and the passengers, including the MacArthurs, alternately stood, sat, crouched or lay on the deck of the plane, packed like matches in a box. The craft shook with the vibrations of the four engines, which occasionally sputtered ominously. The parachutes they wore, and the life rafts they shared space with, made them terribly and constantly aware that death was as close as an enemy aircraft or the sea ten thousand feet below them.

As they climbed from the plane, Mrs. MacArthur announced to Colonel Huff, the general's aide, that she "never, never wanted to get into another airplane." They must, she said, find a way to travel to Melbourne, their final destination in Australia, by land. An hour later she was back on the B-17, despite her determination, taking off just ahead of Japanese bombers.

Their destination this time was Alice Springs, in the same Northern Territory as Darwin, but more than eight hundred miles southward and almost exactly in the center of Australia. There was a little-used railroad from Darwin to Alice Springs, Colonel Huff found, but it went only part of the way. The road was only a trail. As he was gathering these details, Huff and others of the party were alerted that Japanese bombers were headed for the field.

Told only that they must rush to make connections in Melbourne, and thus maintain the General's schedule, Jean MacArthur was hurried aboard one of the B-17s. She was still protesting as the plane roared down the runway, throwing the passengers off balance before they found places to sit.

It was late in the afternoon of March 17, 1942, when the party arrived at Alice Springs, to learn that the passenger train for Melbourne ran once a week—and they had missed it by one day! The weather was stifling, hot and dry, and the black Australian flies swarmed in the open air and infiltrated the flimsy screens of the Alice Springs buildings.

The transients were put up at the town's one overcrowded hotel and that night, as Colonel Sid Huff related in his *My Fifteen Years with General MacArthur*, they went to an open-air movie where a double feature was advertised. The first film was an old American western, so incredibly bad that the General walked out at the end, although he was an inveterate movie-goer and this was the first one he had seen since leaving Manila for the siege of Corregidor.

A "special train" was arranged for the next day, consisting of a dumpy little engine and tender, two wooden coaches and a caboose. The first car was equipped with wooden benches which ran lengthways of the car. A table had been rigged in the second for dining, while enough food for the three-day trip to Melbourne was stacked in ice-filled tubs at the end of the car. There was no connection between the two passenger vehicles, and when it was time to eat, the engineer was notified, stopped the train and everyone piled off the first car and into the second. Later that day, an ancient sleeper was added to the entourage. The travelers included the MacArthurs, Ah Cheu, Colonel Huff, General Sutherland and Colonel Morhouse, who was an Army physician.

It was a slow trip, sometimes boring, and the black flies had no trouble in keeping up the leisurely pace. There were infrequent stops at infrequent stations for water and coal. At one of these, the stop was lengthened while Colonel Morhouse took a steel sliver from a rancher's eye.

But, at least, the refugees were out of the active war zone and away from pressure. As Jean MacArthur had predicted, the trip gave the General time to unwind, relax and sleep. At Adelaide, the party transferred to a more modern train and on March 21 they arrived at Melbourne, where cheering thousands filled the station and lined the streets to shout a hero's welcome.

It was in Australia that Douglas MacArthur made the declaration which was to become his most famous and, perhaps, one of the most significant ones of World War II.

At Alice Springs, he was informed that a group of newsmen were waiting to interview him. He hurriedly scribbled a statement on the back of an envelope and, before reading it to the reporters, asked particularly that they try to see that it was included in the radio news reports heard by troops still fighting in the Philippines, and by the Filipinos themselves. It read:

The President of the United States ordered me to break through the Japanese lines and proceed from Corregidor to Australia for the purpose, as I understand it, of organizing the American offensive against Japan, a primary object of which is the relief of the Philippines.

I came through and I shall return.

Just as MacArthur's escape was seized upon as one of the rare opportunities for Allied celebration during those disheartening days of the war in the Pacific, so his last sentence became a symbol of hope for the conquered people of the Philippines.

Europe had its "V for Victory" signs scrawled on the walls of every occupied city; MacArthur's "I shall return" became the pledge of faith for the Philippines, there, too, to be emblazoned on bomb-damaged buildings and quoted by the guerrillas in the jungles and hills.

When MacArthur had left Corregidor, knowing finally that help could not come from the United States, he had no other thought but to start immediately the drive back to free the Philippines from the Japanese.

These islands were his second home. His first post when he graduated from West Point in 1903, as a twenty-three-year-old second lieutenant in the Army Corps of Engineers, was the Philippines. He was sent there for a second tour of duty in 1922, and for a third in 1928. After completing his assignment as Chief of Staff, War Department, in 1935, he was invited by President Manuel Quezon to return to the Philippines as Military Advisor of the Commonwealth, to help prepare the islands for military self-reliance. They were scheduled for independence on July 4, 1946.

MacArthur accepted this invitation, serving for some two years in his rank as a four-star general and then, under pressure from political enemies and others jealous of his influence over the Filipinos, he retired in the rank of full general. At that time, the Philippine Assembly, the islands' law-making body, made him Field Marshal of the Philippine Army.

On accepting the Marshal's baton from President Quezon at Malacanan Palace, MacArthur spoke to all the Philippine people:

"The military code has come down to us from even before the age of knighthood and chivalry," he said. "The soldier, above all men, is required to perform the highest act of religious teaching—sacrifice. In battle and in the face of danger and death he discloses those divine attributes which his Maker gave when He created man in His own image. However horrible the incidents of war may be, the soldier who is called upon to offer and to give his life for his country, is the noblest development of mankind."

MacArthur's military plan for the islands was one which disavowed any offensive aims, but which would insure an adequate defense against the predatory tendencies of any other nation. Even then, he was convinced that Japan was building a war machine designed to expand her empire in the Pacific—and that the Philippines would be one of the early targets.

His army was to be small, a hard core of regular troups, supplemented by a reserve force of universal military trainees. The navy was to have a complement of from 150 to 200 motor torpedo boats and the air force from 1,500 to 2,000 fighter and reconnaissance planes and light bombers.

He gave the Philippine people three basic principles which he considered fundamental:

The first is that every citizen is obligated to the nation's defense. No man has the inalienable right to enjoy the privileges and opportunities conferred upon him by free institutions unless he simultaneously acknowledges his duty to defend with his life and with his property the government through which he acquired these opportunities and these privileges.

The second great principle is that our national defense system must provide actual security. Indeed, an insufficient defense is almost a contradiction in terms. A dam that crumbles under the rising flood is . . . a desolate monument to wasted effort.

Third, is the insistent need for current and future economy. Although there are no costs of peace comparable to those that would surely follow defeat in war, it is nevertheless incumbent upon the government to avoid unnecessary expenditure.

MacArthur's adopted countrymen were stirred by his words, but, as in other lands, there were many needs for the national income and the Field Marshal frequently found that, while his program was being extravagantly praised in the halls of government, he was, at the same time, denied the funds to carry it out. He was, moreover, getting little or no help from the United States, which was much more preoccupied with Europe and the war which had started there in 1939.

On July 27, 1941, Douglas MacArthur was recalled from retirement to active duty by President Franklin Roosevelt in the rank of Lieutenant General. He was ordered to muster the Philippine army into the service of the United States as part of the United States Army of the Far East, which he was to command.

By December, when the Japanese struck, MacArthur had been able, with some help from the United States, to put together the small force that was to hold and delay the Japanese offensive in the Pacific for months. It consisted of:

20,000 Filipino regulars and 100,000 reservists in 10 divisions, not entirely mobilized.

19,000 American officers and enlisted men, including Army Air Corps personnel.

200 combat aircraft, of which perhaps 165 were operational. They included 35 newly arrived B-17 four-engine bombers and 100 F-40 fighters.

The naval force in the area was not under MacArthur's command. It was the reinforced Asiatic fleet and consisted of 3 cruisers, 13 destroyers, 29 submarines, 3 submarine tenders, 1 submarine rescue ship and 6 PT boats, with 30 PBY flying boats and 4 seaplane tenders in an air patrol wing.

In the first Japanese attack, ten hours after Pearl Harbor, the Japanese destroyed seventeen of the B-17s on the ground, the others having been removed to Mindanao. The blame for this has been the subject of bitter argument by military historians for more than twenty years now. Since it was his command, MacArthur took the responsibility. Actually, there were several factors involved, including a lack of space on Del Monte Field, at Mindanao, a misinterpretation of orders, and the judgment of junior officers.

MacArthur's plan of defense for the islands, designed at first to hold until reinforcements arrived, and later to simply hold on until his forces were wiped out or overwhelmed, had long been worked out. His Luzon defensive force was split into two principal commands:

The North Luzon Force, commanded by Major General Jonathan Wainwright.

The South Luzon Force, commanded by Brigadier General Albert M. Jones.

There was also a small reserve force directly under MacArthur's control.

The Japanese began their land attack against Luzon on December 10, with landings at Aparri on the north coast and Vigan on the west. Sensing that these were diversionary tactics, MacArthur met them only with aerial defense. Then, on December 22, the Japanese main invasion force of sev-

enty-six transports, supported by battle craft, struck at Lingayen Gulf on the west coast. Two days later, twenty-four
more transports landed troops at Atimonan, Lamon Bay, on
the eastern coast.

"The Japanese strategy became immediately apparent,"
wrote MacArthur. "The Japanese sought to swing shut the
jaws of a great military pincers, one prong being the main
force that had landed at Lingayen, and the other the units
that had landed at Atimonan."

The strategy was intended to divide MacArthur's north
and south armies and to force them into battle before the city
of Manila. But MacArthur had other ideas, long planned.

With the North Force under General Wainwright execut-
ing a holding maneuver, the South Force under General
Jones began sideslipping into the Bataan peninsula for a last-
ditch stand. By choosing Bataan, MacArthur also denied the
Japanese the use of Manila Bay.

The focal point of General MacArthur's plan was the small
Calumpit Bridge, just south of San Fernando at the top of
Manila Bay. There, two spans crossed the swift and treacherous Pampanga River and its bordering marshes. One span
carried rail lines. The other carried the two lanes of the only
major highway leading into Bataan.

If the Japanese got there first, they could divide MacArthur's forces and gobble them up in pieces. To prevent this,
two things were essential: that Wainwright hold back the
Lingayen horde in the North and that the Southern Force
move with almost impossible speed to avoid the trap.

Military transportation was far from adequate for the job,
so the island of Luzon was scoured for every available civilian
vehicle. Buses, trucks, private cars, motor bikes and even
horse-drawn carts were commandeered. They formed endless
columns day and night along the narrow roads, carrying men

and weapons, food, ammunition and supplies—and the line never stopped.

When the enemy discovered MacArthur's maneuver, he threw every available regiment and division in a desperate attempt to cut the line at San Fernando—and ran into the overwhelming fire power of artillery that MacArthur had waiting there.

The battle raged for the final three days. Wainwright would fight a delaying action determined enough to bring up the enemy in full force, and then fall back, dynamiting bridges and roads as he went, to stand again. The last American reserve force, a small tank unit, was thrown into the battle at Calumpit Bridge and held the enemy off with a series of costly counterattacks.

Success came in the term of split seconds. The deadline for demolishing the bridge had been set for 6:00 A.M., New Year's Day, 1942. On December 31, the Japanese commander massed his troups for an intensive assault, only to have them delayed by the tank attack. At 3:00 A.M., the last of the tanks withdrew over the bridge, followed by infantry in trucks— under fire from approaching Japanese riflemen. The last infantryman crossed at 5:00 A.M. Holding off for the return of the demolition men, General Wainwright delayed final action until 6:15 A.M. Then he gave the order and watched as the two spans over the Pampanga crashed into the stream. The withdrawal to Bataan was secure.

The strategy of the maneuver and the success of its execution were hailed by military men all over the world, including the Japanese, as one of the most brilliant in military history. MacArthur followed it by declaring Manila an open city, without military value (although the Japanese bombed it, anyway), and moving his own headquarters to Corregidor, in order to direct the last stand on Bataan.

Bataan has been described by one military man as "a green hell, clotted with fibrous undergrowth, cogon grass, inhabited by pythons and indented by rock cliffs and treacherous rivers." The attacking Japanese were forced to fight their way up the precipitous Zambales Mountains, ranging up to 4,700 feet.

There the heroes of Bataan, both American and Filipino, held off the Japanese invaders until May, 1942, two months after General MacArthur had broken through the lines to take over the command in Australia. By his organization of the Philippine defense, and the brilliance of its execution, MacArthur had tied down massive Japanese military forces on Luzon, broken the momentum of the Japanese drive and dealt a blow to their Pacific invasion schedule from which they never recovered. Shortly afterwards, the General started the great drive by land, sea and air which took him back to fulfill his promise: he had promised "I shall return," and he did. For his Philippine exploits, General MacArthur was awarded the Congressional Medal of Honor, the nation's highest military award. The citation read:

For conspicuous leadership in preparing the Philippine Islands to resist conquest, for gallantry and intrepidity above and beyond the call of duty in action against invading Japanese forces, and for the heroic conduct of defensive and offensive operations on the Bataan Peninsula. He mobilized, trained and led an army which has received world acclaim for its gallant defense against a tremendous superiority of enemy forces in man and arms. His utter disregard of personal danger under heavy fire and aerial bombardment, his calm judgment in each crisis inspired his troops, galvanized the spirit of resistance of the Philippine people, and confirmed the faith of the American people in their armed forces.

2

☆ ☆ ☆ ☆ ☆

THE LEGENDARY courage of the MacArthurs is come by honestly. A thousand years before Douglas MacArthur was awarded the Congressional Medal of Honor, as his father had been before him, their ancestors were ranging the heathered hills of Scotland, sounding the famous battle cry of the MacArthur clan, *"Eisd O Eisd"*—"Listen, O Listen."

On his father's side, Douglas was descended straight from the ancient warriors of the Scottish Highlands, in a line from both his grandfather and grandmother. They were cousins, both named MacArthur.

Legend places the MacArthur clan, like their famous rivals, the Campbells, as descendants of the fifth century King Arthur of the Round Table, through his son, Smervie Mor. Historians trace an alternate lineage back to another Arthur, son of King Aedan MacGrabhran, of Argyll, and his wife, a princess of the ancient British kingdom of Strathclyde, probably eighth or ninth century.

From wherever the clan derived in this Celtic twilight of Scottish history, the antiquity of it has given the Scots a proverb which runs:

"Hills and streams and MacAlpines we know, but when did the MacArthurs come?"

(Kenneth MacAlpin ruled in the ninth century as the first king of the Scots and he was progenitor of the Bruce clan, as well as the MacAlpines.)

The early history of the MacArthurs, like that of Scotland, is fragmentary. There are half-buried stones in memoriam for MacArthurs who died in the crusades. In the thirteenth century, the early members of the clan held extensive lands in the old earldom of Garmoran and were the chieftains over other related branches of the family, probably including the Campbells. History mentions Cheristine, daughter of Alan MacRuarai, a related clansman, who was given a grant of a large tract in Garmoran.

The Scotland of those early days was not only divided geographically into the Highlands and the Lowlands, but these areas were also separated by speech, custom and culture. The Lowlands were largely feudal; the landowner lords ruled their thrifty Scottish peasants and artisans with authority from the kings. They in turn were super-tenants; their rent was paid in fealty and men-at-arms, when necessary. Most of the Lowland folk spoke English.

The Highland chieftains ruled clans and federations of clans. They gave lip service to crown loyalty, but their real authority came from the allegiance of their clansmen, and it was frequently a personal thing. The Highlanders spoke the Gaelic tongue.

The MacArthurs are recorded as a powerful clan as far back as the early thirteen hundreds, when a MacArthur embraced the cause of Robert the Bruce, who brought independence to Scotland during his reign from 1306 to 1329, and whose heroic deeds in those days of chivalry are well recorded in both story and verse.

As warrior favorites of the crown through the reigns of Robert the Bruce, and of his son, David the Second, and their nephews, Robert the Second and Robert the Third (both Stuarts), the MacArthurs prospered. The clan was made Keeper of Dunstaffnage and given lands in Lorne, western Scotland. Later, they added Strachur, and the ports of Glenfalloch and Glendochart, on the shores of Loch Fyne.

During the reign of David II, old records tell of a political struggle between the leaders of the MacArthur and the Campbell clans, when the latter tried to usurp both authority and property. The Campbell, MacCailean Mor by name, lost his claim (and probably his head) when David II decided for the MacArthurs.

The MacArthur septs, or family groups, come to us in written history and legend under varied spellings of the name. There are—in addition to today's MacArthurs—the McArthurs, the MacArthours, the MacAirthours and the Arthurs (from whom American President Chester Alan Arthur probably descended). There are other spellings—MacCartair, MacCarter and MacArtair. They are all believed to have originated from one single source—at some time in Scotland's stirring past.

History tells that a Dougall McAirthour was Sheriff of Argyll in 1595, and that a Dougall McArthour (possibly the same man) was notary at Glenurquhay in 1580. Innis Chonnel Castle, on Loch Awe, near Loch Fyne, was another MacArthur keep in the fifteenth and sixteenth centuries. Inishail, on Loch Awe, is the traditional burying ground of the MacArthurs.

Having reached the height of their power in the Highlands during the thirteenth and fourteenth centuries, the MacArthurs came a cropper in the fifteenth. King James I of Scotland, son of Robert III, had been captured by the English while still a schoolboy. After eighteen years of captivity, during which he had an opportunity to study the powers and peculiarities of English rule, James was ransomed and ascended the Scottish throne.

He devoted much of his time during the thirteen years of his reign to effectively disciplining the Scottish lords, particularly the Highland Chieftains whose strength, influence and independence he considered a threat to the crown. In the early 1430s, he called a parliament of the leading Scottish nobles, and among those who answered the invitation was one John MacArthur.

He is described in the scanty annals of the time as a powerful overlord of the MacArthur and allied clans, the holder of many lands and towns, and he commanded a full thousand fierce fighting men. A lesser leader might have hesitated where he walked in, notwithstanding the promise of safe conduct extended all the chieftains.

Once within the palace walls, MacArthur and several other lords were seized, imprisoned and tried for treason to the crown. Treason in those days took many forms, depending sometimes on the evidence available. It was a flexible term.

With what evidence, or without any at all, is not recorded, but John MacArthur, along with others, was convicted and beheaded. His extensive lands were confiscated, except for minor holdings in Strachur and Perthshire.

In riches and influence, the clan never recovered. As individuals, they were still MacArthurs, with the same characteristics which had always marked them. Members of the family remained for centuries about Dunstaffnage, but they were now tenants of the Campbells. Others became pipers to the MacDonalds, leading their forces into battle. Still others, eventually, emigrated—one to Australia to establish a branch of the family there. Another came to America.

And in Scotland they still quote yet another proverb:

"There is nothing older than the hills, unless MacArtair and the devil."

3

D OUGLAS MACARTHUR and his father, Arthur MacArthur, are the only father-and-son team in history to both hold the Medal of Honor, the nation's highest award for bravery. There were many other similarities in their careers.

The father was an army officer for forty-six and a half years, the son for forty-seven and a half years. The citations Douglas received for bravery on the battlefield in World War I were frequently almost interchangeable (barring time and place) with those written on his father more than fifty years earlier, in the Civil War.

Both served as military governors, both fought over the same territory in the Philippines, both were recognized experts on the Far East and both waged political battles for recognition of the importance of that hemisphere to America. No two members of the same family, in American history at least, have ever before so clearly symbolized military leadership and courage on the field of battle as did this father and son.

The first MacArthur to land on these shores was Douglas MacArthur's grandfather, Arthur MacArthur, who traveled from Glasgow to Boston in 1825, at the age of ten, with his widowed mother, Mrs. Sarah MacArthur. Her husband, the great-grandfather of Douglas MacArthur, was also named Arthur; there has been an Arthur MacArthur in every generation since, on the order of two centuries.

Mrs. MacArthur and her son settled in Chicopee Falls, near Springfield, Massachusetts. The boy attended Uxbridge and Wesleyan Academies and Amherst University, then studied law in New York and was admitted to the bar in 1840. He practiced law in both Springfield and New York, became judge advocate of the Western Military District of Massachusetts and a captain of the militia, his only military connection. In the union of his second marriage, Arthur MacArthur, father of Douglas, was born on June 2, 1845.

The MacArthurs moved to Milwaukee in 1849 and in 1855 Arthur was elected lieutenant governor on the Democratic ticket. While his election was never questioned, that of the governor on the same ticket was contested and proved to be fraudulent. Unable to take the post, the disqualified official named Arthur MacArthur to it instead. In the political and legal turmoil which followed, MacArthur's appointment was held by Wisconsin courts to be illegal. Refusing—as followers urged—to use state troops to hold his office, he turned the post over to his Republican opponent at the end of five days' tenure, remarking:

"In this world there have never been but two kinds of government—a government of force without law, and a government of law without force." It was the first known test of a MacArthur attitude of civil versus military law.

In 1857, after returning to the practice of law, Arthur MacArthur was elected judge of the Second Judicial Circuit, where he served for thirteen years. President Lincoln knew and liked him and President Grant called him to Washington in 1870 to be associate federal judge of the District of Columbia, where he remained some eighteen years. His grandson, Douglas, was born on his sixty-fifth birthday, January 2, 1880. He died peacefully during a visit to Atlantic City on August 24, 1896, at the age of eighty-one. Douglas was then sixteen.

Douglas described his grandfather as "a large, handsome man of fine presence, genial disposition and marked charm of manner." He wrote also that his grandfather taught him many card games, including poker. On one occasion, having taken young Doug's last chip away from him by laying down four kings to Doug's four queens, he remarked, "My dear boy, nothing is sure in life. Everything is relative."

Arthur MacArthur, father of Douglas, grew to young manhood in the politically and emotionally stirring days which preceded the Civil War. He idolized Abraham Lincoln and even emulated the Illinois rail splitter's early custom of studying by the light flickering from the fireplace.

He was sixteen when the war started and wanted to join the navy as a midshipman. Convincing Arthur that the art of war, like other professions, requires study before practice, his father sent him to a military academy where he learned the rudiments of tactics and strategy; in fact, he was such an apt pupil his instructors wanted him to attend West Point.

But Arthur was to be restrained no longer. With his father's consent and influence, in August, 1862, he signed up as first lieutenant and adjutant of the 24th Wisconsin Volunteers, composed largely of men also from Milwaukee. Reporting for duty, he looked anything but a soldier. He seemed younger, even, than his seventeen years. He was slim, not particularly strong, and his voice was inclined to break without warning. It was still in the process of growing. His first order, given at drill, brought guffaws of rude laughter from his troops. His colonel muttered into his beard that the governor had sent a boy to do a man's job.

If there was any real feeling about Arthur not being able to do his job, it did not last long. On October 8, 1862, the regiment had its baptism of fire in the battle variously known as Chaplin Hills and Perryville, in Kentucky. The Union forces, commanded by General Phil Sheridan, fought off repeated confederate attacks. Arthur's men said afterward that he seemed to be all over the field of battle, usually where the fighting was thickest. He was cited three times for bravery and coolness under fire. His colonel relied on him without question, and, more important, so did his men. Arthur was breveted to the rank of captain, a form of battlefield promotion then given partly in place of a decoration. Arthur's pay remained that of a lieutenant, however.

After Perryville came the battle of Murfreesboro, in Tennessee—called the battle of Stone River by the South. It started on New Year's Eve and raged three days into 1863. Seasoned now by the earlier battle and several months of rigorous training, the 24th Wisconsin was positioned on the extreme end of Sheridan's division, which held the right of the line.

The regiment pivoted and then wheeled back into position under the repeated Confederate attacks which attempted to turn the flank, but gave not one foot of ground. At the end of the day, the 24th Wisconsin had lost nearly half its strength and every mounted officer was down except the adjutant—Arthur MacArthur. He won further citations in this battle and again was breveted, this time to major.

His greatest battle, and the one in which Arthur MacArthur won undying fame in history, was Missionary Ridge, on November 25, 1863. The Confederate forces under General

Baxton Bragg held the steep, rocky hill, with their first line a row of rifle pits at the foot of the ridge.

General Sheridan was ordered to take the first line of rifle pits, and his men did, stopping there momentarily, confused, exposed to a withering fire from the higher slopes. They had taken their objective; holding it was untenable. They must go forward against tremendous odds, or fall back.

There were no orders, or at least none afterward recalled, but suddenly the colors of the 24th Wisconsin moved forward, borne by the two color guards and the adjutant.

The color guards fell almost immediately and the adjutant seized the flag. He raced forward a few steps until he was surrounded by nothing but the gray coats of the enemy. Then his voice, still high but never hesitant, came back, crying: "On, Wisconsin!"

One of those weird hushes that occasionally fall over the bloodiest of fields of battle hung for a moment over Missionary Ridge. All was quiet for a second, maybe two, maybe five, then Wisconsin came on with a wild roar, followed by the entire division, and Missionary Ridge was won for the North. Writing of it movingly, MacArthur said:

The adjutant falls on the ground, exhausted and retching. He is a terrible sight, covered with blood and mud and filth, hatless, his smoke-blackened face barely recognizable, his clothes torn to tatters. Sheridan just stares at him and then, blood and filth and all, takes him in his arms. And his voice breaks a little as he says, "Take care of him. He has just won the Medal of Honor."

Arthur MacArthur bore, apparently, the same charmed life which marked his son more than fifty years later. He was wounded five times; once a packet of letters stopped a bullet reaching for his heart; bullets passed through his clothes a score of times. A dozen horses were shot from under him.

Following Missionary Ridge, he was made a lieutenant colonel and then colonel, and was given command of the 24th Wisconsin. At nineteen, he was the youngest colonel of the Union Army. In his last battle—Franklin, near Nashville, Tennessee—he was wounded in the shoulder, chest and knee, but led his 24th Wisconsin to victory in taking the objective. He recovered from his wounds in time to lead his regiment home, 334 men and 25 officers out of the proud 1,000 who had marched away three years earlier.

Colonel Arthur MacArthur was mustered out of service on June 10, 1865, at the age of twenty—still not old enough to vote. He spent almost a year in Washington, D.C., studying law at home under the gentle teaching of Judge Mac-Arthur. But he had seen too much action to be sedentary now. In February, 1866, still not twenty-one, he accepted a commission as a second lieutenant in the 17th Regular Infantry. He was promoted, the same day, to first lieutenant, then to captain, six months later. That marked the end of his rapid promotions. He remained a captain for twenty-three years, which was not unusual in those days.

For the next seven years, Captain MacArthur was a part of the American frontier life which has been the subject of a thousand movies and television shows. These were the days when the Army's chief assignment was that of bringing peace to the Plains Country and the Great West by subduing the Apache and the Sioux. He became the friend of both Buffalo Bill and Wild Bill Hickok when they hunted buffalo for and guided his troops. He lived through the Indian wars of the Utah and Wyoming Territories, where Fort Rawlins, Fort Bridger, Camp Stambaugh, Camp Robinson and Fort Fred Steele were the little-known names of stockaded outposts and the scenes of many a battle between bluecoat and redskin. He survived a dozen ambushes and at least one hand-to-hand battle which had to end in death for one opponent or the other.

A tour of duty in 1874-75 took him to New Orleans where, during Mardi Gras, he met and wooed Mary Pinkney Hardy, one of the seven daughters of Dr. and Mrs. Thomas Hardy of Norfolk, Virginia, who also had seven sons. "Pinky" Hardy's mother had been Elizabeth Margaret Pierce, and on both sides of her family, Pinky was descended from Revolutionary settlers and Southern colonists who had fought under General George Washington and General Andrew Jackson and General Robert E. Lee.

The Hardy background was one of spreading plantations, benevolent slave ownership, hoop skirts and crinolines. The family home was a stately mansion known as Riveredge. It sat on the banks of the Elizabeth River, in the community of Berkley, now a part of Norfolk. Riveredge is now a state-maintained MacArthur memorial, and General Douglas MacArthur is buried there.

Captain Arthur MacArthur and Pinky Hardy were married at Riveredge on May 19, 1875. Four of Pinky's brothers, who had fought in the Confederate Army, registered passive objection by not attending the wedding.

Captain and Mrs. MacArthur's first son was born in 1876, a year after the wedding and the same year, incidentally, that General George Custer made his last stand against Sitting Bull at Little Bighorn. (It was about the only dramatic military moment of the era that Arthur MacArthur missed.) The boy was named the traditional Arthur, making, at this point, three Arthur MacArthurs in the family—son, father and grandfather. Malcolm, the second boy, was born in 1878 and Douglas two years later, January 26, 1880, at the old Arsenal Barracks in Little Rock, Arkansas.

Five months after the birth of Douglas, Captain MacAr-

thur and K Company of the 13th Infantry were transferred to
Fort Wingate, in New Mexico, where all three of the boys
contracted the measles and Malcolm died of the illness. A
year later, K Company moved again, this time to Fort Seldon,
a tiny adobe military outpost near El Paso, Texas, and the
Mexican border.

(Later records show that Douglas MacArthur also survived
diphtheria, scarlet fever and mumps, the almost normal child-
hood diseases of that day.)

Captain MacArthur's assignment was to guard the fords of
the shallow Rio Grande River, which separates the United
States and Mexico, against the attacks and depredations of
Geronimo, the Apache chieftain whose life span stretched
from 1829 to 1909 and who contrived to make the lives of
white settlers miserable through a good share of it.

It may have been duty for the military, but it was a small
boy's dream for young Douglas. He learned to ride before
he could read, and to shoot side-winding rattlesnakes which
abounded on the sandy trails and low hills. It was an era of
cowboys and frontiersmen on the American side of the river,
and vaqueros on the Mexican, while the Indians—peaceful
Navajos and Hopis, in addition to the constantly warring
Apaches—knew no international boundaries as they rode their
ponies and burros over the land. There were covered wagons
and pony express riders on the trails, and tall tales from
travelers to listen to around the fire at night, tales of outlaws
and Indians and the heroic derring-do of that day. They were
stirring and heady times for the young son of a famous
soldier who had already made up his mind to follow in his
father's footsteps.

In 1889, Arthur MacArthur was promoted to major and
stationed in Washington, D.C., as assistant general. Along
the way, the family had spent one tour of duty at the newly

organized Army school in Fort Leavenworth, Kansas, where Douglas faced his first regular school with daily classes. His mother had been tutoring both of the MacArthur boys, since there were no schools in the western army outposts.

The result was somewhat dismal and, even in Washington, where Douglas completed his grade schooling, his marks were average or less. The other male members of the family did better. Major MacArthur attended night school in Washington and received his Doctor of Laws degree in 1889, at the age of forty-five, while son Arthur won an appointment to the Naval Academy at Annapolis in 1892. (Arthur, a Navy captain, died in 1923 after a brilliant career in the Boxer Rebellion and World War I, winning both the Navy Cross and the Distinguished Service Medal. His death from a ruptured appendix was a severe and sad blow to his brother Douglas.)

To the great delight of his son Douglas, Major MacArthur was posted to Fort Sam Houston, in San Antonio, Texas, in 1893, so the boy was back in his beloved West. Here, also, Douglas was able to enroll in the newly established West Texas Military Academy (now the Texas Military College) and school took on a new meaning for the youngest MacArthur. His obsession with a military career led to a fascination for knowledge. Subjects which had been dull suddenly became interesting; his grades went from bad to good and then to best in the school. While he still delighted in riding and hunting, and with turning his vacations into the ranch life of the cowboy, he also discovered school athletics. He played on both the football and baseball teams, and was the school tennis champion. Later on, Douglas MacArthur looked back on these days as the happiest in his life.

In the spring of 1896, Arthur MacArthur's promotion to lieutenant colonel and his assignment to the Military Department of the Dakotas, in St. Paul, Minnesota, coincided with another event: the Congressman from Milwaukee, where the MacArthurs maintained legal residence, announced a competitive examination for a West Point appointment the following year. After a family consultation, it was decided that Douglas should try for it. He and his mother moved to Milwaukee, where they lived in a private hotel while Douglas attended high school. His father commuted weekends from St. Paul.

With his mother's constant encouragement and help, young Doug worked harder than he ever had in his life, spending days in class and nights and weekends poring over his books. When the examination was held, he led all the contestants and won the coveted appointment. He entered West Point on June 13, 1899. Looking back, it was a momentous day for this country and for history.

Arthur MacArthur, at this time, found himself engaged in another war, the course of which was as much of a surprise to him as it was to the American people at the time. It was the Spanish-American War of 1898. As a result, the United States acquired Cuba and the Philippine Islands, plus Hawaii, rather incidentally.

Since Cuba was only ninety miles off the Florida coast, the average American in those days had a pretty good idea of its location. He also, however, was apt to assume that the Philippines, being likewise Spanish, were nearby—and not ten thousand miles away. When the battleship *Maine* was sunk in Havana Harbor, following highly inflammatory stories in the American press about the Spanish treatment of the Cubans, war was declared.

Prior to this declaration, orders had been sent to Admiral Dewey, in the Pacific, to proceed immediately and, in case of hostilities, to destroy the Spanish fleet in Manila Bay. The orders were secret and, apparently, had been sent earlier by Theodore Roosevelt, then Assistant Secretary of the Navy, without consulting his superiors in the Navy, or elsewhere, including the President.

Steaming undetected past the same Corregidor from which Douglas MacArthur escaped forty-four years later, Dewey sank the Spanish fleet without the loss of a single American life. This action thoroughly confused several million people back home, who weren't sure as to what or where the Philippines were—nor what we were doing there. But, as quickly as amazement died, it was replaced by a strong public movement to keep what we seemed to have acquired. Recovering his aplomb, President McKinley bowed to the "public will," and the United States entered the global political arena. Army troops were sent to support Dewey.

With them went Arthur MacArthur, newly promoted to Brigadier General and shortly thereafter given the second star of a Major General and command of the Second Division. Young Douglas wanted to volunteer immediately, but his father prevailed upon him to continue his career toward West Point. There would be other wars, he said prophetically.

The Treaty of Paris eventually ceded the Philippines to the United States (with the payment of $20,000,000), but no one had consulted the Filipinos about their feelings in the matter. They had been quite happy to help the Americans drive the Spanish completely off the island. But when they found that the United States intended retaining sovereign power over the now-liberated land, they objected strenuously to exchanging one set of masters for another, and General Arthur MacArthur had a brand-new war on his hands.

The Filipinos rallied behind the leadership of a fiery young revolutionist, Emilio Aguinaldo, and Arthur MacArthur found himself facing a situation that was almost the parallel of one that his son was to confront nearly fifty years later—fighting an all-out war with too few forces and too little equipment to win it. Finally reinforced, although with still only about half the strength of the opposing Philippine Army, General MacArthur conceived and executed a series of brilliant maneuvers in North Luzon which routed the enemy and sent Aguinaldo into hiding.

MacArthur then executed perhaps the most brilliant maneuver of all. He discovered the location of Aguinaldo's hideout, surprised and captured him. But, instead of throwing the idol of the rebels into prison, MacArthur brought him to his own quarters, installed him in a comfortable room and treated him as a guest—although still a prisoner.

He then invited insurgent lieutenants, under a flag of truce, to visit their leader, his honored guest. One who did so was a then Major Manuel Quezon, who later became President of the Philippine Commonwealth and who shared the dangers of Corregidor with another General MacArthur forty-four years later. Aguinaldo informed his followers, through Quezon, that he had taken an oath of allegiance to the United States. The war ended.

General MacArthur became military governor of the Islands and, before his rule was supplanted by civilian authority, won the hearts and friendship of the Filipinos by the creed he laid down for the preparation of the Island for independence.

"The idea of personal liberty allows a citizen to do within limits whatever tends to his own happiness," he said. "That idea we are planting in the Orient. Wherever the American flag goes, that idea goes.

"The fruition of that idea in the Philippines is merely a matter of evolution and, to my mind, a brief one. The Filipinos want (and need) precisely what we can give them.

People ask us what we are going to accomplish in a money way. The planting of liberty—not money—is what we seek. The human race has propagated its higher ideals in a succession of waves, and now its waves are passing beyond the Pacific."

Arthur MacArthur established the first free public school system and replaced the Spanish medieval code of law with one based on modern civil procedure. He set up bureaus of roads, harbors and railroads, established a civil service and laid the basis for a system of national defense. Years later, Quezon, as President, paid him a tribute:

"The American to whom we owe most is our first military governor, Arthur MacArthur. He conquered us in war but his greatest victory was his conquest of us in peace."

And, in 1945, as General Douglas MacArthur stood on the reviewing platform in the great victory parade which marked his return to the Islands and defeat of the Japanese invaders, he spied the graying but erect figure of Emilio Aguinaldo marching in the forefront of the Philippine guerrilla forces. He whispered an order to an aide, who disappeared and then returned, bringing Aguinaldo. Douglas MacArthur placed him by his side on the stand for the remainder of the ceremonies.

The Generals MacArthur, father and son, not only had, each of them, a well-developed sense of the dramatic, but drama seemed to seek them out. Arthur MacArthur, after capturing Aguinaldo, did not casually imprison him; he placed him in the seat of honor at dinner, and his opposition capitulated.

When Douglas MacArthur reached Australia after his escape through the lines from Corregidor, he didn't tell newsmen that he hoped in the course of the war in the Pacific to free his Filipino friends from the Japanese; he said, "I shall return," and his words became a rallying cry of the campaign.

The death of Arthur MacArthur was a dramatic final act for this old soldier, one that few writers would have dared put into a play.

He left the Philippines a Lieutenant General, at that time the highest rank in the American Army, but the play of politics of the day blocked his assignment to be Chief of Staff. Instead, Arthur MacArthur was assigned to his home state of Wisconsin, "for such duties as may arise." In 1909, he retired at the age of sixty-four, with forty-six years of service as an officer in the United States Army behind him.

On September 5, 1912, his old comrades of the 24th Wisconsin Regiment scheduled a reunion at the University Building, in Milwaukee. There were only ninety left of the one thousand who had volunteered fifty years earlier. General MacArthur at first declined an invitation to participate. His health had been uncertain; his physician had advised against it. Then, two principal speakers, including the Governor of Wisconsin, canceled their attendance because of the extreme, unseasonal heat, so, on the pleadings of old friends, Arthur MacArthur arose from his bed for his last military duty. He had once said:

"My country has granted me every privilege except that of dying at the head of my troops."

On this eventful September 5, he stood on the platform, once again before "his troops," speaking to them:

"This may be the last opportunity," he told them, "I shall ever be offered to pay homage to you, my comrades."

Then he stopped and his hand went to his heart. "Comrades, I am too ill to go on," he said, and slipped backward to the floor.

The regimental surgeon rushed to his side . . . and arose a moment later to say, "Comrades, the general is dying."

The men in the audience knelt by their chairs and began reciting the Lord's Prayer. When it ended, Arthur MacArthur was dead.

Captain Edwin Parsons, who served as Regimental Adjutant, the same position MacArthur had held fifty years before when he joined the Regiment, and who had been at MacArthur's side in a score of battles and skirmishes, took the Regiment's battle-torn American flag from the wall and draped it over the General's body. As he gazed down at his leader's body, he, too, collapsed. He followed his commander in death two weeks later.

4

WHEN Douglas MacArthur entered West Point in 1899, at the age of nineteen (he had had to delay a year due to a spine ailment which cleared up completely), he was a striking mixture in character, behavior and thinking, of his father and mother.

It would be difficult to say, even from this distance in time, which had the greater influence on both the boy and the man. Douglas MacArthur idolized his father, copied his mannerisms and appearance, grew up under the influence of his attitudes, and wanted nothing better than to follow in his footsteps. He adopted his father's impeccable manners, his unfailingly courteous demeanor and speech; like his father, Douglas read extensively and could talk interestingly, accurately and fluently on widely varied subjects. Both were religious, but kept their beliefs apart from their public lives, except in statements or speeches. Both were sticklers for accuracy.

Mary MacArthur, the mother, was a woman of strong will and determination. As a girl, she had been a great beauty; as a woman, she was handsome, poised, cultured and indomitable. She had a clear and unshakable sense of right and wrong, and, once having decided between whites and blacks, there was no room for gray areas. Like his mother, Douglas was able to make up his mind, to form his opinions, with unshakable firmness. Mary MacArthur's selection of friends for herself, and her approval or disapproval of friends for her son, including the feminine variety, were based on personal standards rarely compromised. Douglas MacArthur's measure of friendship, or perhaps personal acceptance is a better phrase, was based upon equally strict standards—usually focused on performance.

General George Kenney, MacArthur's air officer during the Pacific War and today, at seventy-five, as tough and unsinkable as when he fought his way back to the Philippines with his commander, island by island, said of him:

"He was a terrific guy to work for. Once he found you knew your job and could do it, he let you alone. And when he believed in you, Mac would back you up against anybody. He was a good friend."

It would be impossible for three such strongly willed people as these MacArthurs not to have had enemies and detractors.

Arthur MacArthur, the highest-ranking military officer in the Army, was denied an appointment as Chief of Staff and relieved of any substantial duties because of a feud with William Howard Taft, later to be Secretary of War and then President, which began when Taft replaced him as Governor of the Philippines.

Mary MacArthur has often been accused of wielding an overly great influence on her son's life, of affecting his first (and unsuccessful) marriage, and of keeping him single throughout a good share of his prime manhood.

And Douglas MacArthur, despite his position as perhaps the greatest military leader and idol of our times, had many bitter detractors who deplored his "arrogance, vanity and supreme self-confidence" and—perhaps—his success. He, too, incurred the displeasure of a President—Harry Truman—and was relieved of his military duties.

With these mixtures of character and behavior acquired from his father and mother, plus an extremely bright mind, a fine intellectual capacity, good study habits and a compelling determination to excel, Douglas entered West Point. He stood just over seventy inches tall, weight 134 pounds, was black-haired, tanned, ramrod-straight and good-looking.

An "Army brat," he was at ease in these stern military surroundings as he signed himself in, that June, 1899, and wrote: Born: Little Rock, Arkansas, Little Rock Barracks, Pulaski County, January 26, 1880. Schools: 3 years public school; 2 years private school; 4 years normal school; 2 years private study; 3 months special preparation for West Point."

Two things set Douglas MacArthur apart from his fellow cadets when he began life at the Point:

His father was probably the most famous general officer in the American Army and he was much in the news, due to the Spanish-American War and his exploits in the Philippines.

His mother moved to West Point with him and spent all four years in Craney's Hotel, just off the Academy grounds. Neither of these things made Douglas' life any easier during his first plebe year which, in those days, was almost notoriously rough, in any event.

From Mrs. MacArthur's point of view, the move was logical. Her husband was ten thousand miles away, in the Pacific. Her elder son had graduated from Annapolis and was on sea duty with the Navy. Craney's Hotel was a rambling, ramshackle structure (Lafayette had stayed there in post-Revolution days), but it was near the only member of the family she had left in the country. Nor was she the only cadet mother there; Mrs. Ulysses S. Grant, mother of Cadet Ulysses S. Grant III, was at Craney's a good share of her son's four years in the Academy, too.

Nevertheless, there is no doubt that Douglas suffered a great deal of raillery because of his mother's presence and often heard the term "mama's boy." Even in later years, when enumerating the number of "firsts" Douglas accumulated during his four years at the Point—first in class, first captain, etc.—it was considered permissible to also add: "And the first cadet whose mother went through West Point with him."

If Douglas ever regretted for one moment his mother's being there, it was never shown. They had always been close; she had tutored him in the early frontier post days, when there were no schools, and her strong will had guided many of his decisions. He saw her every day, either slipping away for a brief visit at the hotel or, if unable to get off the post, they would stroll back and forth in front of the barracks for thirty minutes in the evening.

He was accustomed to discussing his problems with her— and always did throughout her life—on equal terms. In choosing a course of action, even in minor matters, Douglas normally talked the matter out with his mother before making a determination.

His first roommate at West Point was Arthur P. S. Hyde, a first classman. Hyde's rooming arrangements had gone awry and he asked Douglas if he would like to join him. Young Douglas excused himself politely, dashed to the hotel and discussed the proposal with his mother. Returning to Hyde a few minutes later, he accepted, thanking him courteously.

Mary MacArthur was a gracious lady and it took her only a few months to win the friendship of many of the cadets. Before the end of the year, she was accepted and even appreciated as a welcome addition to the rather stark social life of the Point. One time, as MacArthur related years later, when he and another cadet were visiting her—without formal permission to be off the post—the hotel desk sent word up that the Academy Superintendent had come to call. Douglas and his friend scurried to escape in the only way open to them—down a back stairs to the cellar and out a dust-blackened coal chute—while Mrs. MacArthur received her distinguished guest in unruffled serenity.

The custom of hazing the plebes or fourth classmen by the upper class cadets had grown unchecked at West Point until, by that time, it had long since passed reasonable limits. Begun originally as a means of instilling the rigid discipline of the soldier into the raw plebes, it had been permitted to develop into actions that, at times, amounted to sadistic brutality.

The sons of illustrious fathers were particularly singled out. Sometimes, Douglas MacArthur, in the mess hall with a forkful of food on the way to his mouth, would be halted and required to recite in detail his father's exploits. Philip H. Sheridan, Jr., frequently found himself galloping astride a broomstick up and down between rows of tents at summer camp, crying, "Turn, boys, turn; we're going back," in mockery of his father's famous rallying cry at the battle of Winchester, Virginia. Ulysses S. Grant III, came in for his share of similar torment because of his noted forebear.

But these were only the innocuous forms of the hazing practices which reached their high, or perhaps low, point in 1889, the year Douglas MacArthur was a plebe. The details did not become public until a year later, via two investigations into the cause of the death of Cadet Oscar L. Booz.

Cadet Booz entered the Academy in the class of 1898 and was the victim of severe hazing. He became ill before the end of the school year and, as his health continued to deteriorate, resigned in October, 1899. He died December 3, 1900, and, as a result of accusations that his death was due to brutal treatment at the hands of fellow cadets at the Point, on December 11, Congress passed House Resolution 307 to investigate.

The report of the investigation went into great detail about the fine art of hazing as it was practiced among the cadets, particularly on MacArthur's class.

Plebes, it noted, were known as "beasts" and their quarters as the "beast barracks." There was no friendship between the plebes and upperclassmen, no social intercourse. Any plebe must obey any order of any upperclassman at any time. The plebe must not be seen smiling or laughing, but on the other hand, he must not be sullen, either.

He was frequently called upon to perform duties for an upperclassman, such as cleaning his room, his gun, his bayonet or sword, taking out and returning his laundry, or making his bed. These, too, the Congressional report noted, were minor matters, but it listed, in addition, more than one hundred distinct methods of harassing the plebes which had been worked out by ingenious upperclassmen over the generations. The report divided them into three classes:

1. Hazing purportedly for the good of the men or service.
2. Punishment for violations of the Upper Class Code.
3. Hazing for pure amusement.

The report called attention to the fact that much of the hazing, including the so-called "Upper Class Code" (an unwritten set of rules for plebes in their relationship with upperclassmen), was illegal, but was permitted with the tacit or unwitting consent of Academy officers. The report also defined a number of the one hundred "methods of harassing," including these:

Bracing: Ordering a plebe to stand in an exaggerated attitude of attention. It only becomes punishment, of course, when the duration is great. An hour was not unusual, although some of the plebes fainted before their time was up.

Eagling: This entailed the victim leaping into the air, arms and legs outflung, then falling to the ground as an eagle swooping on its prey. It might have been good clean fun a dozen times. The Congressional investigators found one hundred was normal and four and six not unusual.

Wooden Willying: Standing with the rifle at "ready," lifting it to the position of "fire" and return, one or two hundred times.

Doing Footfalls: In this exercise the plebe lay on his back with his legs extended rigidly over his head. The legs must then fall, still rigid, to the ground and be raised again—and again and again and again.

Choo-chooing: This maneuver entailed the plebe lying on his back and working his arms and legs in imitation of a steam locomotive.

Push-ups and Knee Bends: These were the simpler exercises.

Stretching: Hanging from a tent bar, legs drawn up, for a prescribed period of time or until the unhappy plebe dropped from exhaustion.

Soirees: Mass hazing of any type.

Hot Sauce: The West Point mess served a South American bottled sauce, known by the cadets as "hell sauce," which was several degrees hotter than the usual chili pepper concoctions. Various doses, taken with a spoon, were prescribed by upperclassmen for plebes. (One such dose was claimed to have led to the throat ailment contributing to the death of Cadet Booz.)

Qualifying: This related to forced feeding, i.e., ordering

the plebe to stuff himself with an inordinate amount of anything from prunes to cabbage to lemon cream pie.

Sliding on Soaped Floor: Naked. Splinters.

Standing on Head in Tub of Water: This became even more "sporting" when the plebe was ordered to recite something while his nose and mouth were submersed.

Cold Bath: The plebe ran, minus clothing, through a gantlet of upperclassmen, who tossed buckets of cold water on him.

Paddling: Naturally.

The investigating committee took into account that many of the above hazing stunts could be harmless if conducted in moderation, but found they usually were not. The report read:

It is of course impossible to determine . . . just what has been the effect of this long course of cruel and annoying treatment on fourth classmen. We do know that several of them, notably Cadets MacArthur, Brith and Burton, were hazed into convulsions and that many others were hazed until they fainted.

The committee also took official cognizance of the custom of "fighting." Any cadet who refused or failed to obey an order from any upperclassman, under the Code of the Upper Classmen, was "called out" for a bare knuckle battle.

Each upper class had, the committee found, a "fighting committee." Any case of plebeian disobedience was placed before the "fighting committee" of the upperclassman involved and a judgment was made as to guilt. If guilt was judged, a member of the committee was selected to call the offending plebe out for a fight. An effort was made to select an upperclassman whose height and weight reasonably coincided with those of the plebe. The committee thought that any degree of fairness ended there; since the upperclassman was a member of the committee, he probably was fairly well versed in fisticuffs. And, while the fight was carried out under the Marquis of Queensberry Rules, all of the seconds and the referee were upperclassmen.

Neither antagonist, the committee found, could or would avail himself of the privilege of throwing in the towel. The bare knuckle battles were fought until one or the other participant was insensible or too weak to stand. Testimony showed that the loser, and frequently the winner, too, usually went to the hospital for treatment at the conclusion. In about four out of five cases, incidentally, the winner was the upperclassman.

Concurrently with the Congressional investigation, President McKinley and Secretary of War Elihu Root ordered a Board of Inquiry (Special Order 290, dated December 11, 1900) into hazing at the Point. The Board consisted of General Officers of the Army and its President was Major General John R. Brooke.

The Board investigation, like that of the Congress, centered on the class of 1899. One of the witnesses questioned most closely was Douglas MacArthur. Preliminary questioning had revealed that he had been one of the foremost victims. When asked why, an upperclassman (who had not participated) replied, "I suspect it is because he is the son of General Arthur MacArthur."

Douglas MacArthur has related many times the soul-searching ordeal he went through during the testimony. He was, as a cadet, under military orders and military law. Called before the Board of General Officers, he was expected and required to answer all questions.

This he did, in relationship to the hazing itself, the methods, the frequency. Once he was required to do knee bends until he had convulsions; he had been required to recite his father's exploits for hours—which he didn't mind doing, incidentally; he had been exposed at one time or another to every form of hazing; he had many times stood in a brace for an hour at a time; he had never been called out for a fight.

Then the questioning narrowed to one particular incident in which MacArthur had been the subject. He described it in detail and fully. Then came the question he had been dreading, "Who were the upperclassmen?"

It was a direct order. Refusal could mean court-martial, being stripped of his beloved uniform, dismissal from the Academy, the end of life itself, as far as Douglas MacArthur was concerned.

His decision had been made days before, reached after long discussions with his mother, who gave him, perhaps, the courage to carry it through. He refused to divulge the names of his tormentors, then pleaded for mercy for himself.

The matter was not pursued. He was not punished. Life went on.

As a result of the inquiries, hazing at the Point was sharply curtailed. Almost twenty years later, as Superintendent of the Academy, Douglas MacArthur almost completely ended the practice.

MacArthur's scholastic record at West Point, 98.14 for the four years, was highest in his class and had not been equaled in—and here the record differs. Some say one hundred years; MacArthur himself says twenty-five years. Either is sufficient.

The hazing episodes of his plebe year obviously did not affect MacArthur's studies and he took full advantage of the privilege of rooming with an upperclassman. Plebes were required to have their lights out at 9:00 P.M. Upperclassmen could leave them on until 11:00 P.M. With Hyde as a roommate, Douglas got in two extra hours of study each night.

Throughout his four years at the Academy, young Douglas

competed with three other cadets for top honors. The first year he nosed out Ulysses S. Grant, III, who took second place. MacArthur was first in English, math, drill regulations —in every subject except French, in which Grant led, followed by the others in the class of 136.

MacArthur was first again at the end of his second year. Cadet Charles T. Leeds, of Massachusetts, was second; Cadet Harold C. Fiske of New York, third; while Grant had dropped down to fourth place.

Something went awry for Douglas the third year, 1902. It may have been what college students of today refer to as the "Junior Slump." In any event, Fiske and Leeds led the class, while MacArthur dropped to fourth and Grant to fifth place.

If it was a slump, 1902 saw the end of it. In his final year, Douglas MacArthur led all the rest with that remarkable four-year average. Leeds was second, Fiske third, and Grant had dropped to sixth. Douglas also held the post of First Captain, the highest of cadet military ranks.

It is not strange that Douglas MacArthur's classmates remembered him well in the later years of his career. He was one of the first of Class '03 to be assigned to a coveted general staff position in Washington. In 1914, he was recommended to receive the Medal of Honor for a hazardous and valorous exploit in Mexico. He organized, named and eventually commanded the Rainbow Division in World War I as one of the Army's youngest general officers. He married a wealthy widow. He was striking in appearance, a brilliant and effective officer.

The recollections of his associates are generally pleasant and favorable. Despite his "highest" marks, he was not considered a grind. His dress was always immaculate, but he was never thought of as foppish. He had his share of "skins" for infractions of the Point's rigid regulations: "Late at forma-

tion for drill," "Not returning book to library at proper time,"
"Shoes not blacked at formation of guard detail," "Handkerchief on table at police inspection" and so on. They ranged
from fourteen "skins" during his first year to eight in his last.
The most frequent was "Late at breakfast formation."

He was generally popular and well liked, with perhaps a
recognition of future accomplishment. Certainly he himself
did not lack self-confidence. He always intended to be first
in his class and to be chief of staff, and said so.

By and large, Douglas was liked as a serious, intent but not
dull young man. His roommate during his last two years,
Cadet George Cocheu of Brooklyn, remembers MacArthur's
complete absorption in his studies, once started. There was no
conversation, no idle chatting. Although he reputedly was
engaged to a record eight girls at one time and he himself
relates escaping a "skin" for being caught kissing a girl on
Flirtation Walk, Cocheu does not recall that Douglas ever
received or wrote a love letter during their two years as room-
mates.

As he was usually the first to admit, MacArthur's prowess
as an athlete was not outstanding, although he could hold his
own with the average. But making a West Point team was
part of a well-rounded career at the Academy and thus another necessary objective for him. He had played football,
baseball and tennis at his Texas prep school, but after some
assessment of his size and weight, and the competition involved, he chose baseball for his field of endeavor.

He played on the varsity for two years—his second and
third. His record for his first year on the team was one base
on balls, one run, no hits, no errors. The Cadets' first game
with the Midshipmen at Annapolis in 1901 found him playing left field and being subjected to an unmerciful razzing
from the middies in the bleachers. Much of the harassment

was based on their doubt of his ability, particularly as opposed to that of his famous father.

His revenge came late in the game, with the score tied 3 and 3, and with 2 outs. MacArthur came to the plate, worked the count up to 3 balls and 2 strikes and then to 4 balls for a walk.

What young Mac lacked in skill with the bat, he made up in speed, and with the next pitch he broke for second. The Navy catcher, already upset over what he considered a rankly unfair call on MacArthur's last ball, threw wild and the ball got away from the second baseman.

MacArthur streaked on for third and the throw which might have caught him went over the third baseman's head, with Mac trotting in to score. It was one of the few times in baseball history when a walk was virtually stretched into a home run, and it proved to be the deciding run of the game. The Navy stands were strangely silent when MacArthur again took the field.

He won another "A" during his third year and then became team manager. It was a job requiring skills more suitable to his ability and still permitted him to travel with the team.

Douglas MacArthur was graduated on June 11, 1903, top man in his class, first captain, first man to receive his diploma, a second lieutenant of the then elite Corps of Engineers.

In his address to the graduating class, Secretary of War Elihu Root, told the new officers, "According to all precedents in our history, before you leave the Army you will be engaged in another war. . . . Prepare your country for that war."

5

S ECOND LIEUTENANT Douglas MacArthur's first assignment
after graduating from West Point was to the Philippines.
He spent his graduation furlough with his father and mother
in San Francisco, where General Arthur MacArthur was
commanding, and then reported to the Third Battalion of
Engineers at Manila. The voyage to the Orient took thirty-
eight days.

For the Philippines and the new lieutenant it was a case
of love at first sight. He found the climate, the Latin culture
and the people, both men and women, charming, and they in
turn found the tall American, in their own phrase, *muy
simpatico*. He met officials who knew, respected and admired
his father. Among his first acquaintances were two young
Filipinos, Manuel Quezon and Sergio Osmeña, destined to
be first and second Presidents of the Commonwealth, although none of them dreamed of it at the time. He began
tutoring in the Spanish language, an item noted on later
records.

MacArthur's duties were typical of those delegated to a
junior engineering officer and that he performed them well is
noted in his efficiency report of "excellent" for the assign-

ment. He helped build harbor improvements, pier and dock buildings on most of the islands. One of his jobs was overseeing the construction of fortifications on the island of Corregidor. Another was to survey the Bataan Peninsula, that fermenting, green jungle where his combined American and Philippine forces held back the Japanese forces in 1942.

The peninsula of Bataan is thirty miles long and fifteen miles wide at its northern or land end. Its western South China Sea coast alternates between sheer drops and shallow shore lines, protected by knifelike coral outcroppings. Corregidor guards its southern tip and a range of rocky, precipitous mountains crosses the northern entrance. Its lowlands are one mass of vine-entangled trees and undergrowth. Rivers and streams with steaming, swampy borders make any progress slow and dangerous. It is a place of pythons and the smaller poisonous tropical snakes, and of every crawling, stinging insect known to man.

In crossing and recrossing every mile of this green horror, MacArthur learned it well—and saw and remembered its possibilities for defense. Amphibious assault from the China Sea was impractical. Guns from Bataan could cover Manila with a deadly fire. Corregidor protected the southern tip, mountains the northern end.

This knowledge of Bataan determined his strategy in 1942. His familiarity with the terrain enabled him to make a hairbreadth maneuver in slipping his forces into Bataan ahead of the Japanese.

It was in the Philippines that the young officer came under fire for the first time. One of his assignments was a repair job on the pier and harbor buildings at Guimaras Island, at the mouth of Iloilo Harbor. Leading a small detachment to cut timbers, MacArthur stumbled into an ambush.

There were two men, one on each side of the trail. Mac-

Arthur drew his service revolver and crouched as a rifle bullet went through the crown of his hat, sent it sailing from his head and cut a small sapling behind him.

Then he dropped both guerrillas, one bullet for each.

A burly sergeant came rushing up the trail, his own weapon at ready, and took in the scene—the two dead men lying by the trail, MacArthur, revolver in hand, a little pale and shaky. The sergeant picked up the still smoking hat and, thrusting one finger through the bullet hole, handed it to MacArthur. Then, with the respect which seemed due, he drew himself up and saluted, remarking in that familiar but deferential third person form which old Army sergeants used to employ, "Beggin' the lieutenant's pardon, but the rest of the lieutenant's life is pure velvet."

MacArthur retold this story many times. It was his baptism by fire.

The year 1904 saw Douglas MacArthur promoted to first lieutenant and transferred from his Philippine post (in October) to serve with the Golden Gate defenses in San Francisco. He had hardly sunk his teeth into the details of the new assignment when the Russo-Japanese War broke out and his father was detailed to Tokyo, as American military observer. Shortly thereafter, Douglas was assigned as General Arthur MacArthur's aide.

Mrs. MacArthur made the trip, too, as far as Tokyo, for the whole MacArthur family was now in the Far East. Douglas' brother Arthur was now a naval lieutenant, stationed at Manila with his wife and young son, the third living Arthur MacArthur.

Douglas arrived in the Orient too late to observe the war, but he did have the opportunity of meeting the Japanese military leaders and of observing at close quarters the Japanese soldiers who had gained an amazing victory over their much larger and—seemingly—much more powerful foe. He was greatly impressed with both leaders and soldiers, and collaborated with his father on a report which pointed up the potential of Japanese ambitions in the Pacific, ambitions which must inevitably be aimed straight at the Philippines. These Islands stood in the path of any route toward conquest. The report echoed General MacArthur's concern that the Pacific, with its forty per cent of the world's population, was the key for any power or combination of powers bent on world domination.

As a result of the MacArthur paper, father and son were ordered to broaden the scope of their observance to the rest of the Orient, with special attention paid to the colonial territories. The trip took nine months and covered Calcutta, Singapore, Peshawar, Bombay, Hyderabad, Bangalore and Rangoon in India, the Crown Colony of Hong Kong, Java, Siam, Indochina and several points in China, including Shanghai.

The two officers were received everywhere with elaborate hospitality and were permitted, to the surprise of Douglas, to inspect military installations and fortifications. They had frank discussions with military and government leaders, saw the good and bad sides of colonialism and brushed bodies with the East's uneducated and underfed millions. Their report at the conclusion of this journey, in addition to its strategic messages, re-emphasized the opinion that the United States, as a great power, must turn its eyes more and more to the Orient in the future.

Toward the end of 1906, back in the United States, Lieutenant MacArthur was assigned as a student at the Engineer School of Application, located at what is now Fort McNair, in southwest Washington. And, on December 4 of that year, Secretary of War William Howard Taft received a letter from the secretary to the President of the United States, Theodore Roosevelt. It read:

"The President directs that Lieutenant Douglas MacArthur be detailed as an aide to assist at the White House functions this winter, such detail not to interfere with some regular work under the Department."

What Secretary Taft thought of the phrase "some regular work" is not known, nor with what emotions he regarded the son of his old foe, Arthur MacArthur, being placed in such a strategic position with the President. Douglas MacArthur notes that the order came as a surprise to *him*.

MacArthur got along fine with Teddy Roosevelt, who shared his interest in the Far East and who was also a friend of General Arthur MacArthur, although the two had differences from time to time. As a White House aide, Douglas came in close contact for the first time with the political greats of that period. Elihu Root had moved from the War Department to be Secretary of State. John D. Long was Secretary of the Navy and Leslie M. Shaw of the Treasury. (Taft was, of course, head of the War Department.) The famous Uncle Joe Cannon, Speaker of the House, was a frequent White House guest, as was Senator Henry Cabot Lodge.

The year 1908 saw Lieutenant MacArthur in Milwaukee, where his father was now stationed, and there he received his first—and possibly one of only two—bad marks on an efficiency report. A Major William Judson, the officer in charge of Doug's engineering outfit, found him "lacking in zeal" and wrote that MacArthur had verbally remonstrated against an order placing him on temporary duty in Manitowac (from Milwaukee). The major was required by regulations to send a copy of his unfavorable report to MacArthur, who protested it vehemently. The correspondence, now in the Archives of the United States, makes a sizable bundle, but it doesn't make clear the outcome, i.e., whether Major Judson saw fit to retract.

(Efficiency reports of that day, incidentally, still called for an evaluation of the officer's swordsmanship.)

The second such incident occurred in 1912, when Lieutenant Colonel W. P. Burnham was noticeably lukewarm in rating Captain MacArthur at Fort Leavenworth, where he was serving as an instructor. The rating could not have been taken very seriously by the Army top brass, however, because in 1913 MacArthur was selected as a member of the General Staff, a group of thirty-eight officers chosen largely as the "brains of the Army."

The assignment was vastly important to Captain MacArthur, because, even as the General Staff's most junior member, the job brought him into intimate contact with the nation's top military leaders and their civilian counterparts in government. It gave him invaluable experience in the do's and don't's of dealing with appointed cabinet leaders and the elected Congress; particularly, he got his first clear insight of the military's never-ending struggle for appropriations.

General Leonard Wood was Army Chief of Staff at the time, and Admiral George Dewey was President of the General Board of the Navy, equivalent of today's Chief of Naval Operations. Douglas MacArthur as a boy had known General Wood when he was busily chasing Geronimo through the hills of the Southwest (winning the Medal of Honor for his bravery) and stopped at Arthur MacArthur's posts. Admiral Dewey was, of course, the hero of Manila Bay. A young Assistant Secretary of the Navy with whom Douglas became fast friends was one Franklin Delano Roosevelt. And, his old *compadre*, Manuel Quezon, was in Washington as a member of the Resident Commission of the Philippines.

The year 1914 saw the United States in its second shooting involvement with Mexico. The Mexican War of 1846, about on a par both morally and militarily with the Spanish American War, brought us great tracts of territory, all paid for legally. Now General Victoriano Huerta, in one of a series of internal struggles for power, had seized such reins of government as existed and needed the excuse of an outside threat to consolidate his power. Americans personally and American property were molested and the heady fever of war again swept America.

President Woodrow Wilson ordered the port of Vera Cruz blockaded, and on April 21, 1914, just a few months before World War I broke out in Europe, American marines seized the port. Their occupancy was followed up by a landing of the Fifth United States Brigade, commanded by Major General Frederick Funston, who had won his first star for capturing the guerrilla leader Aguinaldo for General Arthur MacArthur in the Philippines.

As the Mexican situation became more complicated, the General Staff decided it would be a good idea to send a member to Vera Cruz. His assignment would be to study conditions and report in detail to General Wood and the War Department.

The officer selected, somewhat to his own surprise, was Captain Douglas MacArthur.

6

In the National Archives on Constitution Avenue, in the capital city of Washington, among millions of other documents important to the nation's history, there is a twenty-two-page report prepared half a century ago. Its title is:

> PROCEEDINGS OF A BOARD OF OFFICERS CONVENED TO REPORT UPON THE AWARDING OF A MEDAL OF HONOR TO CAPTAIN DOUGLAS MacARTHUR, GENERAL STAFF CORPS (C.E.), FOR SERVICES IN MEXICO ON RECONNAISSANCE DUTY FROM VERA CRUZ TO ALVARADO ON THE NIGHT OF MAY 6-7, 1914.

The pages of the report relate the deliberations of three Army officers, sitting in judgment as to whether the nation's highest award for valor shall be given another officer for a distinguished act of bravery. The report:

> Proceedings of a board of officers pursuant to the following:
> WAR DEPARTMENT
> Office of the Chief of Staff,
>
> January 21, 1915
> Memorandum for the Chief, War College Division:
> The Chief of Staff directs me to refer the accompanying papers,

relative to a Medal of Honor for Captain MacArthur, to the War College, and to state that he desires it be considered by a board at the War College consisting of Colonel Treat, Lieutenant Colonel Johnston and Major Lockridge.

He desires the report of this board be submitted to him for his action.

Secretary, General Staff.

The Board met at the War College on February 2, 1915, with all members present. From this and subsequent meetings the members prepared a summary and made their recommendations. The summary began:

Major General Leonard Wood (War Department Chief of Staff) was designated by the Secretary of War to command a possible expeditionary force in Mexico and directed to prepare the necessary plan of operations. Captain Douglas MacArthur, General Staff Corps, was to be a General Staff officer of the Commanding General of the expedition.

The latter part of April, 1914, Captain MacArthur was sent by the Secretary of War, upon recommendation of General Wood, from Washington, D.C., to Vera Cruz, Mexico, with general instructions to obtain, through reconnaissance and other means consistent with the existing situation, all possible information which would be of value in connection with possible operations.

Captain MacArthur stated in his report to General Wood:

"On arrival at Vera Cruz, the headquarters of the Fifth Brigade did not recognize me as an official member of their command, as I had no orders assigning me thereto. They took the attitude that I was an independent staff officer functioning directly under you. I was permitted to exercise my own judgment in regard to fulfilling my general orders and instructions, subject to only such limitations as were prescribed by the Military Governor for all those domiciled in Vera Cruz.

"In undertaking this reconnaissance, therefore, I was thrown entirely on my own responsibility, as it was not feasible or safe to communicate the question to you for decision. The object of the trip not being aggressive, but merely for the purpose of obtaining information, my general instructions as given above seemed to cover the very contingency, and I accordingly made my plans."

Shortly after he arrived at Vera Cruz Captain MacArthur (had) heard through a Mexican railroad employee that a number of engines of military value were hidden somewhere on the line connecting Vera Cruz and Alvarado.

The latter place is about forty-two miles southeast of Vera Cruz. Captain MacArthur hired three Mexican railroad men to assist him in a trip to obtain definite information about the matter. At this time Captain MacArthur was not a member of General Funston's command at Vera Cruz. In his report, Captain MacArthur states "Captain Cordier, of the 4th Infantry, was the only person outside of these men (the three hired Mexican assistants) who knew of the plan."

At dusk, May 6, 1914, Captain MacArthur, in uniform, left our outposts about Vera Cruz. He proceeded on foot to a hand-car manned by one of the hired Mexicans outside of our outpost line. He traveled on this car without incident to Boca del Rio, but at the Jamapa River found the railroad bridge down.

The car was left here concealed, the river crossed in a rowboat, and the journey continued on two ponies to the vicinity of Paso del Toro, near which place the other two Mexicans with another hand-car were found waiting according to previous arrangement. The trip from here to Alvarado was made with the hand-car and the three Mexicans, two of the Mexicans taking the car through towns while Captain MacArthur, with the other, went around to avoid detection.

Shortly after one o'clock that night Alvarado was reached and five engines found and inspected. The party then returned about as it came. On the trip Captain MacArthur fought bands of Mexicans that endeavored to stop him at Salinas, Piedra and near Laguna.

On May 19th and August 18th, 1914, Captain Constant Cordier, 4th Infantry, wrote to General Wood regarding this matter stating in part, "If any deed of daring merits the Medal of Honor surely MacArthur's audacious undertaking is one."

On November 25, 1914, General Wood reported the details of the matter to The Adjutant General of the Army, stating that "Captain MacArthur displayed great gallantry and enterprise, and I believe that the service performed clearly entitles him to a Medal of Honor, and I recommend that one be awarded him."

Under date of January 13, 1915, General Funston endorsed General Wood's letter of recommendation as follows: ". . . Until after the return of the expeditionary force from Vera Cruz, and the entire severance of my connection therewith, I had not the slightest information regarding the reconnaissance made by Captain MacArthur. As a matter of personal opinion I should say that the risks voluntarily taken and the dangers encountered were of a most exceptional nature, and that the awarding of the Medal of Honor would be entirely appropriate and justifiable. . . ."

Under date of January 25, 1915, Captain William G. Ball, 16th Infantry, wrote to the Chief of Staff about this matter as follows:

". . . At the time of the reconnaissance I was an aid-de-camp upon the staff of General Funston who was in command of our forces at Vera Cruz. Captain MacArthur was not a member of our command, being engaged on certain confidential work under the direct orders of the War Department. Through me, however, as the personal representative of the Commanding General, he kept in touch with the Command.

"I learned of the reconnaissance immediately after its accomplishment, . . . I am thoroughly familiar with all the conditions surrounding the reconnaissance and unhesitatingly pronounce it one of the most dangerous and difficult feats in Army annals. I was impressed then, and am now, that this officer clearly earned a Medal of Honor, and so expressed myself at the time. I believe a grave injustice will be done if such action is not taken."

The last law of Congress regarding the Medal of Honor (Act

of April 23, 1904, 33 Stats., 274) provides for Medals of Honor:

". . . to be presented by direction of the President, and in the name of Congress, to such officers, noncommissioned officers and privates as have most distinguished, or may hereafter most distinguish, themselves by their gallantry in action, . . ."

Paragraph 182, Army Regulations, 1913, reads as follows:

"Medals of Honor authorized by Congress are awarded to officers and enlisted men in the name of Congress for particular deeds of most distinguished gallantry in action.

"In order that the medal of honor may be awarded, officers or enlisted men must perform in action deeds of most distinguished personal bravery or self-sacrifice above and beyond the call of duty so conspicuous as clearly to distinguish them for gallantry and intrepidity above their comrades, involving risk of life or the performance of more than ordinarily hazardous service, and the omission of which would not justly subject the person to censure as for shortcoming or failure in the performance of his duty. The recommendations for the medal will be judged by this standard of extraordinary merit, and incontestable proof of the performance of the service will be exacted. . . ."

The Board members then took up the requirements of the Medal of Honor and MacArthur's exploit. Their examination and dissection, more briefly told than in the report, said:

The entire reconnaissance could rightfully be called an "action," as required by regulations.

His conduct in initiating and voluntarily undertaking an expedition at night to a vicinity where he was almost certain to encounter hostile forces merited the award.

While it was impractical to get eyewitnesses' testimony to the action, the Board freely accepted Captain MacArthur's report as accurate and truthful.

But, unknown to MacArthur, General Funston had issued orders which "proscribed any member of the reinforced brigade from going beyond the lines" and ordered further that "nothing was to be done that might lead to a resumption of hostilities."

Had Captain MacArthur been attacked in the vicinity of the outposts, either going or coming, hostilities might have been precipitated.

And, while Captain MacArthur acted in good faith, and, while General Funston might have permitted the reconnaissance had he known of it, the fact remained that he was the commander and he was not informed.

After due deliberation and in full light of the above considerations, the Board concluded:

Captain MacArthur's "distinguished gallantry in action" consisted in making the reconnaissance at the risk of his life. But the board questions "the advisability of this enterprise having been undertaken without the knowledge of the commanding general on the ground."

Captain MacArthur showed "distinguished personal bravery beyond the call of duty . . . involving risk of life and performance of more than ordinarily hazardous service." To bestow the award recommended might encourage any other staff officer, under similar conditions, to ignore the local commander, possibly interfering with the latter's plans with reference to the enemy.

If a condition of armistice actually existed, the board questions the policy of awarding a medal of honor for "distinguished gallantry in action" which very action may have been, even though General Funston and Captain MacArthur may not have been informed of this armistice, a technical breach of the terms of armistice, depending upon what kind of military enterprise was expressly prohibited.

While Captain MacArthur could not be criticized for breach of an armistice of the terms of which he was not officially informed, still award of a medal might be ratification by the government of the breach of an armistice the terms of which were known doubtless, by the proper representative of this government.

It is recommended that the Medal of Honor be not awarded to Captain Douglas MacArthur, General Staff Corps, for his service on the reconnaissance from Vera Cruz to Alvarado, Mexico, on the night of May 6-7, 1914.

The two ranking officers on the Board, Colonel Treat and Lieutenant Johnston, signed the report. The third member, Major Lockridge, wrote a minority report. He also recommended against the award but did not, he said, find MacArthur's "action" on his reconnaissance either extraordinary or unusual; nor did he find anything in the combat involved "as clearly to distinguish him for gallantry and intrepidity above his comrades."

MacArthur's own story of the reconnaissance, told in a report to General Wood and now in the Archives, is retold here in his own words:

1. This report is supplementary to the general one made to you under date of May 9, 1914.

2. The general purpose of the reconnaissance was the location of locomotives suitable for road use on the narrow gauge line of the Inter-Oceanic Railroad. Due to the great shortage of animal transportation the command at Vera Cruz was practically immobile. Freight and passenger cars were in abundance, but no road motive power. Every effort was being made to remedy this state of affairs so that in case of field operations, which appeared imminent, the command would not be tied to Vera Cruz.

3. Through the maudlin talk of a drunken Mexican, I received an inkling that a number of engines were hidden somewhere on the line connecting Vera Cruz and Alvarado. This man was sobered up and found to be a railroad fireman and engineer on the Vera Cruz and Alvarado railroad. He consented, after certain financial inducements had been offered, to assist me in accurately locating the engines.

4. At this time I occupied at Vera Cruz a unique and rather difficult status. I had been ordered there before the Fifth Brigade

left Galveston as one of the prospective Assistant Chiefs of Staff of the First Field Army. My orders were defined in a letter from the Secretary of War to the Secretary of the Navy under date of April 23, 1914, in the following words:

"I am very desirous of sending down for purposes of observation and reconnaissance a representative of the War Department. This officer is Captain Douglas MacArthur, of the General Staff, who, in case of any aggressive movement by the Army in regard to Mexico, will function as one of the General Staff Officers of the Commanding General. In order to facilitate his observations and his passage to Vera Cruz, I would appreciate very much if the Admiral Commanding be requested to extend such privileges to him as may be possible, and that the Battleship "Nebraska" which it is expected will touch at New York tomorrow be directed to take him on board as a passenger."

On arrival at Vera Cruz, the headquarters of the Fifth Brigade did not recognize me as an official member of their command, as I had no orders assigning me thereto. They took the attitude that I was an independent staff officer functioning directly under you. I was permitted to exercise my own judgment in regard to fulfilling my general orders and instructions, subject to only such limitations as were prescribed by the Military Governor for all those domiciled in Vera Cruz. In undertaking this reconnaissance, therefore, it was thrown entirely on my own responsibility, as it was not feasible or safe to communicate the question to you for decision. The object of the trip not being aggressive, but merely for the purpose of obtaining information, my general instructions as given above seemed to cover the very contingency, and I accordingly made my plans.

5. The Alvarado Railroad is a narrow gauge road connecting Vera Cruz and Alvarado, distant about forty-two miles. The principal towns en route are Tejar, Medallin, Paso del Toro, Laguna, La Piedra, and Salinas. We held the line as far as Tejar, nine miles out. About four miles beyond Tejar, at Paso del Toro, the

Alvarado line is crossed by the broad gauge line connecting Vera Cruz and the Isthmus of Tehuantepec. This latter line, after leaving Vera Cruz, passes through the town of Boca del Rio, where it crosses the Jamapa River, before reaching Paso del Toro. From Vera Cruz to Paso del Toro, therefore, these two railroad lines formed roughly the two halves of an ellipse. We did not hold the Isthmus line beyond the outskirts of Vera Cruz.

6. Mexican troops in force were reported near Tejar and in order to avoid them I determined to proceed along the Isthmus line as far as Paso del Toro and then change to the Alvarado line. My general plan was to leave Vera Cruz alone on foot at dusk and to join my Mexican engineer who was to have a hand-car in waiting outside of our outpost lines. Thence we were to proceed to Paso del Toro where he had arranged to have a narrow gauge hand-car on the Alvarado line manned by two Mexicans. From there we were to push along the line until the engines were located and their condition ascertained. All three of the Mexicans were railroad men and their affiliations and experience enabled them to obtain the hand-cars and have them at their appointed places. For their services I agreed to give them $150 gold, payable only after my safe return to Vera Cruz. Captain Cordier of the 4th Infantry was the only person outside of these men who knew of the plan.

7. The night was squally and overcast. At dusk I crossed our line unseen near the wireless station, where a detachment of the 7th Infantry was encamped. I was in military uniform with no attempt at disguise and with absolutely nothing on me in addition to my clothes except my identification tag and my automatic revolver with ammunition. I found my engineer with a broad gauge hand-car in the appointed place. I carefully searched him, and after some demur on his part removed his weapons, a 38 caliber revolver and a small dirk knife. As a further precaution against his possible treachery, I had him search me so that he might better realize that there being nothing of value on me my death would afford him no monetary return. The essence of the trans-

action for him, therefore, became my safe return to Vera Cruz when he would receive his pay.

8. We proceeded as far as Boca del Rio without incident, but at the Jamapa River found the railroad bridge down. I decided to leave the hand-car, concealing it as well as possible. After searching the bank of the river for a short distance, we discovered a small native boat by means of which we paddled across, landing well above the town so as to escape observation. On landing we located, after some search, two ponies near a small shack and mounted on them we followed the trail along the railway until near Paso del Toro. We then made a detour and hit the Alvarado line below the town. The two Mexican firemen were awaiting us with the hand-car. We secreted our ponies and after I had searched the two newcomers and found them unarmed we pushed on. Mile after mile was covered with no sign of the engines. The line is studded with bridges and culverts and my crew protested violently at crossing them without investigating their condition. Time was so short, however, that I dared not stop for such steps, and had to take them in our stride. I was obliged to threaten my men to the point of covering them with a revolver at the first bridge, but after that I had no further trouble with them. In fact, after getting into the spirit of the thing their conduct was most admirable. At every town we reached I took one man and left the car which was run through to the far side by the other two. I fastened myself by a lashing to the man acting as my guide so as to insure us against separation and together we made a circuit of the town joining the car on the far side. This took time, but was the only way I could avoid detection.

9. We reached Alvarado shortly after one o'clock and there found five engines. Two of these were switch engines and worthless for our purpose. The other three were just what we needed— fine big road pullers in excellent condition except for a few minor parts which were missing. I made a careful inspection of them and then started back.

10. At Salinas, while moving around the town with one of my men as described above, we were halted by five armed men. They were on foot and wore no uniforms. They were not soldiers and were evidently one of the marauding bands that infest the country with brigandage as a trade. We started to run for it and they opened fire and followed us. We outdistanced all but two and in order to preserve our own lives I was obliged to fire upon them. Both went down. I was fearful lest the firing might have frightened away my hand-car men, but after some search we found them awaiting us about a mile beyond the town.

11. At Piedra, under somewhat similar circumstances and in a driving mist, we ran flush into about fifteen mounted men of the same general type. We were among them before I realized it and were immediately the center of a melee. I was knocked down by the rush of horsemen and had three bullet holes through my clothes, but escaped unscathed. My man was shot in the shoulder, but not seriously injured. At least four of the enemy were brought down and the rest fled. After bandaging up my wounded man we proceeded north with all speed possible.

12. Near Laguna we were again encountered and fired upon by three mounted men who kept up a running fight with the hand-car. I did not return this fire. All but one of these men were distanced, but this one man, unusually well mounted, overhauled and passed the car. He sent one bullet through my shirt and two others that hit the car within six inches of me, and I then felt obliged to bring him down. His horse fell across the front of the car and on the track, and we were obliged to remove the carcass before proceeding.

13. At Paso del Toro we abandoned the hand-car, found the two ponies where we had left them and made the rest of our way back to Boca del Rio, where we returned the animals from whence we had procured them.

14. We found the boat where we had left it and started to cross the Jamapa River, but when near the shore the boat struck a snag in the darkness and sank. Fortunately the water at this point

was something less than five feet deep, for in our exhausted physical condition I do not believe we would have been capable of swimming. As it was I was hard put to it to keep my wounded man's head above water. Day was breaking when we reached the bank, but so wearied were we that we were unable to move on for nearly half an hour. We then located our first hand-car and ran in close to Vera Cruz where we crossed the American lines unobserved.

15. None of the men we encountered were Mexican troops. All were guerillas undoubtedly bent on general mischief. Owing to the darkness I was not recognized as an American soldier and in consequence no alarm was ever felt for the engines.

7

☆ ☆ ☆ ☆ ☆

Triggered by the assassination of Archduke Francis Ferdinand, heir to the Austrian throne, on June 28, 1914, at Sarajevo, Bosnia, the smoldering political conflicts of Europe broke into the open flames of World War I.

By the end of August, the Central Powers—Germany and Austria-Hungary, allied with Turkey and Bulgaria—had invaded neutral Belgium and were arrayed against England, France and Italy on the Western Front and against Russia on the Eastern Front. (Japan had also declared war on Germany.)

True to its tradition of noninvolvment in European affairs, the United States remained neutral for almost three years. Then, on February 1, 1917, Germany declared unrestricted submarine warfare, with the intent of choking off supplies, including food, to England. It was a move which would inevitably lead to attacks on American ships. The United States broke diplomatic relations the following day and on April 6 declared that a state of war existed between the two countries. On December 7, the United States government took similar action against Austria.

Douglas MacArthur was just thirty-seven when the war

began, a major and a junior member of the Army General Staff. When he returned to the United States from active duty in Europe, two years later, he was a combat-wise Brigadier General, twice wounded. He had been awarded the Silver Star *seven* times and the Distinguished Service Cross twice for heroism under fire. He also held the Distinguished Service Medal for brilliance, skill and judgment as a commander. He had been recommended for the Medal of Honor and for promotion to Major General (action on which was stopped because of the Armistice).

He had also organized and named the Rainbow Division, served as its first chief of staff, commanded its 84th Infantry Brigade and finally the Division itself.

With the declaration of war in 1917, and the need of raising a large armed force as quickly as possible, the Army General Staff found itself sharply divided as to how this should be accomplished. The majority were in favor of a large national army built around the nucleus of the regular army. The minority, and a very small minority it was, believed strongly in using the National Guard units of the various states. The leader of this small faction—recalling that the Guard had performed very well for his father in the Philippines—was Major Douglas MacArthur.

He campaigned for his view to the point where his military superiors virtually ordered him to desist—then he carried it to Newton D. Baker, Secretary of War. After he had convinced Baker, the two of them went to President Woodrow Wilson, and MacArthur's eloquence won out there, too.

Later, when Secretary Baker asked the Major how they could best put his plan into effect, MacArthur replied that very few states had guard units of effective division strength and that it would be a good idea to combine expediency with a symbolic beginning.

"Let us combine units from as many states as possible," he said, "so that this one division will stretch over the country like a rainbow."

The next day, while briefing the press in his job as War Department censor, MacArthur repeated his statement to a group of reporters, explaining that the division existed only on paper and had not been given a number designation.

"Stretching over the country like a rainbow," repeated one of the writers. "The Rainbow Division. That's a good enough name for me." And so it became, although later it was also designated the Forty-second Division.

Secretary of War Baker chose Brigadier General William A. Mann to command the Rainbow and Douglas MacArthur to be its first chief of staff, promoting him from major of engineers to colonel of infantry, on August 5, 1917, for that purpose.

The Rainbow Division listed component units from twenty-six states and its twenty-seven thousand men—infantry, artillery, engineers, cavalry, support and supply—were assembled at Camp Mills, near Garden City, on Long Island, New York.

There MacArthur put his green troops through a schedule intended to fit them for battle. There were no leaves and few passes for officers or men. There were hours of close order drill to establish discipline and to knit the diverse units into one cohesive organization. There was endless bayonet practice and range firing until the soldiers came to feel the army rifle was a third arm. Men from Iowa, Indiana and Wisconsin marched side by side with men from Virginia, Georgia and Texas. When ships were ready and supplies complete, the division was ready. On October 18, 1917, it sailed from Hoboken in a great convoy, flanked by destroyers on the alert for enemy submarines.

Their destination was St. Nazaire, well below the Brittany peninsula on the French coast. The convoy commander was then Naval Captain Yates Sterling, Jr., aboard the *Lincoln*. He wrote of a typical convoy incident thus:

"No man aboard will soon forget the two hours that vessel was stopped in the war zone east of longitude 20 degrees, to repair a disabled air pump. The troops were all at their abandon ship stations with life preservers adjusted. The gun crews were alert, and all lookouts on their toes to discover a periscope. The rest of the convoy swept on and quickly disappeared beyond the horizon. A lone destroyer remained, circling about the huge vessel at high speed. The two hours seemed an eternity. Possibly there was not a submarine within a hundred miles, yet one might have been near enough to make an attack and, if so, six thousand men would have been set adrift five hundred miles from land, mostly on life rafts to which they could only cling, and with the water temperature fifty degrees. There were only six destroyers altogether guarding the convoy. If all six performed rescue work they could not accommodate with standing room all of the shipwrecked men on this one big ship, and to perform this act of mercy they must desert the remainder of the convoy they were guarding and seek port at full speed."

The repairs to the *Lincoln* were made and it caught up with the other ships. Shortly before reaching St. Nazaire, the convoy dodged seven subs successfully and made its way safely into port. The *Covington*, on which MacArthur sailed, was sunk eight months later in another convoy.

The men of the Rainbow disembarked in a drizzling rain but to a joyous welcome from the French residents. The doughboys were as glad to put foot on solid ground as the French were to see them. The Americans marched off the ships singing "Over There," "Keep the Home Fires Burning" and "There's a Long, Long Trail Awinding." After a period of that confusion which seems normal to any military campaign, during which division units were scattered, their reserve supplies were pirated by other divisions and many of their officers requisitioned by higher headquarters, the Rainbow was settled in billets along the Meuse Valley, in eastern France.

By personal appeal to General Pershing's chief of staff, an old friend, MacArthur had avoided another threat, that of seeing the Rainbow split up into replacement units for other divisions in an American Corps.

(The Division commander, General Mann, was nearing mandatory retirement age and he was replaced by Major General Charles T. Menoher, a West Point classmate of General Pershing. MacArthur, of course, remained as chief of staff.)

General Pershing, at this time, was having troubles of his own. The Russians had made a separate peace, thus releasing hundreds of thousands of Austro-Hungarian troops from the Eastern Front, to be added to the armies already facing the French and British on the Western Front. With the Allies desperately needing help, General Pershing adamantly refused to alter his conviction that the American troops must fight as an American Army under American leaders.

Four regiments of the Rainbow were, however, attached to the French troops for battle training and moved, in late February, 1918, into the Luneville-Baccarat combat sector. It was to be the Americans' first taste of trench warfare, of ankle-deep mud, rain, snow, vermin, blood, wounds and death in this, one of the coldest winters in French history. They went on patrols, they engaged in light but deadly raids and they learned the thunderous horror of artillery barrages and to face the waves of attacking Germans which followed.

One of the first such raids came on March 5, on the Chamois center of the lines. It was held by the 168th Iowa Regiment, once commanded by General Arthur MacArthur, father of Douglas. John Taber, in the regimental history, wrote:

A nervous burst of machine gun fire, the boom of a grenade down the line, the crack of a rifle, the distant crowing of a rooster, alternately strike the ear; then for a moment an air of peace and profound silence, broken only by the soft blowing of the wind, envelops this small corner of Lorraine. It is half past four—an hour until dawn.

Suddenly, with the instantaneity of a lightning flash, the whole north seems to rise up in flames and hurl itself forward—like an agile, hungry tiger leaping down upon its prey. With a thunderous, dismaying roar it falls upon the Chamois, raining steel and destruction. There is no need to waken any one; air and earth tremble with the concussion of bursting shells, and men at the front, in the support, back in town, all find themselves on their feet without being conscious of the force that placed them there.

In the trenches every post, save those of the lookouts, is instantly abandoned. Terrified bodies come rushing, slipping, stumbling, splashing to the dugouts, dodging bits of flying debris, ducking showers of dirt, their path lighted by flashing explosions. Already the wires connecting the front with the reserve are out, and all communication is suspended. From each G.C. (*Groupe de Combat*) rockets shoot heavenward, to be answered almost immediately by the alert artillery—half French, half American. Guards at dugout entrances breathlessly watch and wait, eyes and ears strained for the slightest variation in the deafening turmoil that may signify a shift in the barrage and give warning of the approach of the enemy.

Soon the bombardment resolves itself into one steady roar in which it is impossible to distinguish the individual detonation. The heavy concentration of enemy shells is turning the whole Chamois system into a hetacomb of horror and confusion. Trenches that were cease to be and leave in their place gaping

craters which in turn are torn afresh. Carmine flashes from the
northern sky translate themselves into carmine splashes and pools
on the furrowed soil. A heavy cloud of smoke and dust, like a
gigantic pall to enshroud those torn bodies whose spirits have
fled, obscures the waning moon.

Awed and shaken, the men crouch in the dark, oppressive
dugouts, waiting for the signal which will send them forth to
determine their fate. An attempted jest, a bit of forced laughter,
falls unheard from the lips of a comrade, for the pounding of the
guns is only equalled by the pounding of their own hearts and
the heavy breathing of their trembling bodies. A sickening sensa-
tion thus to be caged helpless like a hunted animal which awaits
only the finishing stroke. At any moment one of the larger shells
may bury them all—or they have the alternative of forsaking the
inadequate shelter and being blown to pieces in the open trench.

The barrage (Taber's account goes on) continued un-
abated for half an hour. Then, shortly after five, as the cold
dawn broke, the barrage shifted, and the commanders led
their men back to their post. From behind them, the counterbarrage opened up as the Americans braced for the assault.
They, as did their leaders, knew the German command had
learned these trenches were manned by Americans and this
was a deliberate test, an attempt to demoralize.

G.C. 11 jutted out into No Man's Land, exposed on three
sides, and it was this point the Germans selected for their
principal assault. Their object was to cut off, surround and
overwhelm it. The waves of gray-clad storm troopers followed the barrage. Taber's account goes on to describe this:

Six of them, guided by a line of tape previously laid to mark
their point of entry, reached one of our dugouts just as its four
occupants started up the steps. Without the slightest warning a
grenade burst in the midst of the Iowans and hurled them all to
the bottom. One was killed, the other three wounded.

Three other Iowans rushed up, killed one of the Germans and drove the others off. Similar action was repeated at other points of G.C. 11. One group of doughboys fought off a frontal attack and then had to turn, with seconds to spare, and battle an assault from the rear.

There were many American casualties in this baptism of fire—nineteen killed and twenty-two wounded. One direct hit destroyed an artillery piece and wiped out its entire squad of seven.

For several days the attacks continued, up and down the line, desperate probes to test the mettle of the green American troops. They made mistakes, they lost lives needlessly, but every rising sun saw them still in position, more battle-wise. They won the admiration of the veteran French, troops and commanders alike.

Colonel Douglas MacArthur, too, had his initial "brush" with the enemy in the same sector, winning, thereby, his first Silver Star and the French Croix de Guerre. Staff officers, particularly the higher-ranking staff officers, did not usually go on patrols, so when MacArthur approached the French Commander, General de Bazelaire, for permission to accompany a French raiding party, the Frenchman raised a questioning eyebrow.

"I cannot fight them if I cannot see them," said MacArthur, and General de Bazelaire gave him the authorization.

After daubing their faces black to lessen the chances of reflection, the patrol crawled through the barbed wire and across the muddy shell holes and debris of No Man's Land. MacArthur was beside the French noncommissioned officer leading the party as they neared the German trenches.

A German guard heard them and fired, shouting the alarm. It spread down the trenches in a rattle of machine gun fire.

Flares lit up the whole area as the patrol leaped into the trenches.

The purpose of a patrol raid is to bring back prisoners for identification (to see what units are in the sector) and for any information which may be squeezed out of them. The work is personal and intimate. The raiders must contact the enemy at close quarters, induce those who will to surrender and kill or scatter the rest. It must be done quickly and efficiently, before help for the foe can arrive—because there can be none for the patrol.

The battle in the trenches this night was savage and short and it ended with a grenade tossed into the dugout where the remnants of the German unit had fled. MacArthur and the French poilus took their prisoners and crawled back to the friendly lines.

There the French received MacArthur with open arms, high praise and cognac. General de Bazelaire pinned a Croix de Guerre on the American colonel. Equally enthusiastic, the American command added the Silver Star.

MacArthur's action that night in going out with a French patrol before his own troops were even in the battle, set the pattern he was to follow throughout the war. The MacArthur figure became almost as familiar to the fighting men of the Rainbow as their own officers did. He seemed always around, walking the trenches, checking equipment, making personal reconnaissance jaunts into enemy territory and leading attacks.

His uniform was as unorthodox as his front-line activity (again, for a high-ranking staff officer). He refused to wear a helmet or carry a gas mask. Except on patrols, he carried a riding crop instead of arms. He frequently wore a turtle-neck sweater, usually with a long woolen muffler, a gift from his mother. This latter was no affectation. He suffered from almost chronic throat infections. Frequently aggravated by mustard gas, compliments of the Germans, he was constantly ill or in severe pain, a fact which he successfully concealed most of the time.

He showed absolutely no fear in any situation. He felt strongly that his presence in the front lines, particularly marked by the MacArthur unarmed nonchalance, was a good morale factor for his troops. When an aide or brother officer remonstrated with him for not wearing a helmet, he replied, "I think the best thing that could happen to the American Army would be to have a general killed in action."

After several days in the trenches under more or less constant fire, and participating in patrols and repulsing raids, the Rainbow men who had been detailed with the French for battle training were deemed sufficiently experienced to conduct a raid of their own. Two companies of the 168th Regiment, because of particularly stalwart records, were selected to lead the attack—"F" Company under Captain Casey and "M" Company under Captain Ross.

Colonel MacArthur had requested and been granted permission from General Mencher to lead the attack. He joined Captain Casey and "F" Company for the jump-off. The Regiment's history recounts:

During the anxious wait for the zero hour, Colonel MacArthur, the Division Chief of Staff, arrived at Captain Casey's post. From the first, "F" Company was exposed to the raking deluge of shells, and as the shelters were scarcely shrapnel-proof, the only place to find protection was close to the front walls of the trenches.

Captain Casey noticed shells falling with great regularity just over a trench into which twenty-four of his men had been crowded; so he shifted this detachment and just in the nick of time for they had hardly cleared when the gunners corrected the range and obliterated the trench.

The history does not mention whether MacArthur was with Casey at that moment. If so, the Captain probably saved the Chief of Staff's life also.

When the whistle blew at zero hour, MacArthur yelled in Casey's ear, over the thunder of the bombardment, "All ready, Casey?" Then over the top he went, with the yells of the men who followed a welcome sound.

The regiment's history has more to say:

When Company "F" went over the top, it had in its midst an unexpected guest in the person of Colonel MacArthur. He wore no distinctive uniform, and, as he was unknown at that time to most of the men, he was addressed as "Buddy" or "Say you," and treated as one of the crowd.

One of the men in talking with a friend later said, "I saw a guy with a turtleneck sweater and a cap on and I couldn't figure what a fellow dressed like that could be doin' out there. When I found out who he was, you could have knocked me over with a feather."

It is not customary for staff officers to join in on a party of this kind, but this adventure on the part of Colonel MacArthur was typical of the man; he preferred to learn from actual experience rather than from some one else's reports. It was for such as this that the officers and men under him admired and respected him then and later when he became commander of the 84th Brigade.

The Rainbow's first attack had been eminently successful. They had maintained faultless discipline, hit the Germans hard, taken several prisoners and returned with a minimum of casualties. The battle was known as the Salient du Feys.

As its aftermath, the three leaders, Colonel MacArthur and Captains Casey and Ross, were all awarded the Distinguished Service Cross. The French commander's official report of the action said:

The American officers and soldiers conducted themselves superbly, rivaling our own in dash. In spite of the bombardment of the assembly places during which they suffered losses, they maintained their coolness, and at the zero hour proceeded to the assault with the most splendid bravery.

At this juncture of the war the Germans, using the troops which had been withdrawn from the Eastern Front, launched a massive assault against the British-held sector some one hundred and seventy-five miles from the Baccarat area. Facing a desperate need, the French troops which had been holding the Bacarrat-Luneville line were withdrawn to help the British, and the Rainbow Division was moved in, becoming the first American Division to hold down a sector alone.

MacArthur said later, as related in *The History of the Rainbow Division:*

"The raid of Casey's and Ross's companies of the 168th Iowa, was a test planned by the French High Command to determine what was the mettle of our troops. It was a blood test.

"It was not only a test of the 42nd Division, but also of the American-citizen soldier. It was the first offensive operation of American troops on the Western Front in which companies acted as whole units. It turned out to be the first time Americans ever fought their way into the German trenches.

"I considered this raid of such paramount importance to the future of the Division that I decided to accompany one of the companies myself. The Germans had apparently sensed the raid because they began a counter preparation artillery fire before we got started. The way the men behaved under that fire made me know that they would go ahead and carry out their duty with great determination. They did it—proving that the American citizen-soldier would fight and that the Rainbow was a first-class combat division."

Consequently, the Rainbow units, after a few days' rest, moved right back, many of them, into the same trenches they had vacated, plus those of the French forces. They held them

eighty-two days, during which time MacArthur, his turtle-
neck sweater and his long woolen muffler became commonplace sights in the muddy trenches and dugouts. . . . On June
26, 1918, he was promoted to Brigadier General and placed
in command of the 84th Brigade of the Rainbow Division.

During their eighty-two continuous days in the Baccarat
trenches, the Rainbow's losses were 60 killed, 45 died of
wounds and 971 wounded. The Rainbow also lost its first
prisoners, a total of seven, all taken while on patrol—none in
their own territory. Army General Order No. 50, signed by
the commander of the Sixth Army Corps, cited the Rainbow
for its great fighting qualities and singled out MacArthur for
his "brilliant direction" of the Rainbow staff.

The next few months were the most crucial of the war and
they saw the tide finally turn in favor of the Allies. This was
in large measure due to the American forces which were
pouring into France in a steady stream of arms and men.
When the Rainbow, with its 27,000 men, reached Europe in
November, 1917, it had been the second division to arrive.
By July, 1918, the strength of the American Expeditionary
Force was 40,487 officers and 833,204 enlisted men, com-
prising a vast army which would expand to well over a million by the end of the summer. It equaled, and more, the
German and Astro-Hungarian divisions which had been
thrown into the Western Front by the peace with Russia.

Late in June, it became apparent that the German high
command was about to launch a major offensive on the plains
of Champagne, in an effort to split the French and British
armies and strike again for Paris. On July 4, with less than
two weeks' rest after their siege at Baccarat, the Rainbow
was sent by forced march to join the Fourth French Army,
twenty-five miles west of the Verdun battlefield of 1916. The

Division was inserted into the center of the French line, before the town of Suippes.

There it came under the command of French General Henri Gouraud, *le lion d'Afrique,* who had subdued a large part of Africa for the French and who had been in command of the Fourth Army since 1915. He was wounded three times in the Soudan, once by an arrow. He was shot through the shoulder in the Argonne Forest in 1915 and literally blown into a tree while helping the British capture the Dardanelles from the Turks six months later. One arm and part of a leg were amputated. MacArthur termed this unsinkable bearded hero the greatest of all the French commanders—a general without a weakness.

General Gouraud's battle order to the French and American troops under his command as they faced the desperate attack of the massed German troops was uniquely and typically his own. Dated July 7, 1918, it read:

We may be attacked at any moment.

You all know that a defensive battle was never engaged under more favorable conditions.

We are awake and on our guard. We are powerfully reinforced with infantry and artillery.

You will fight on a terrain that you have transformed by your work and your perseverance into a redoubtable fortress. This invincible fortress and all its passages are well guarded.

The bombardment will be terrible. You will stand it without weakness.

The assault will be fierce, in a cloud of smoke, dust and gas.

But your positions and your armament are formidable.

In your breasts beat the brave and strong hearts of free men.

None shall look to the rear; none shall yield a step.

Each shall have but one thought: to kill, to kill, until they have had their fill.

Therefore, your General says to you: "You will break this assault and it will be a happy day."

General Gouraud had worked out a technique of defense which was to be devastatingly successful against the Germans. With the knowledge of an attack coming, arrived at from captured prisoners and other intelligence, he withdrew his forces from the front-line trenches, stationing them in lines one to two miles in the rear. In the area between the deserted front lines and those manned, he left "suicide pockets" of outposts, who would give warning of the approach of the German attackers, put up what battle they could and then—when possible—escape.

As a result, the enemy artillery barrage would fall into empty trenches and the waves of attacking Germans would have to stumble through two miles of open ground before meeting a determined and surprising resistance that was still intact.

With reasonably firm knowledge that the attack would come on the morning of July 15, the day following French Bastille Day, and with an artillery barrage due to start at midnight, Gouraud withdrew his forces and laid down a tremendous counterbarrage at 11:30 P.M., the night of the fourteenth.

The French used one thousand batteries, pouring tons of exploding steel into the enemy positions for thirty minutes, momentarily knocking the Germans off balance. At midnight, there was a lull, and for ten minutes the French and American leaders wondered if their intelligence had been wrong— if they had been shelling empty positions instead of troops massed for attack.

Then at 12:10 A.M., the Germans opened up with two thousand batteries, twice the strength of the French array and the greatest artillery barrage in history. The roar from the throats of the big artillery pieces stretched along the forty miles of the front, reaching Paris one hundred miles away. The Parisians left their homes to stand in the streets, watching the glow which lighted the whole western sky.

MacArthur awaited the German assault from the Rainbow's main line of defense. At exactly 4:17 A.M., he saw the red rockets go up from the old front lines where a few lonely, heroic sentries had been left. At this signal, the light field guns took over the bombardment. Their shells covered No Man's Land, keeping pace with the advancing Germans.

The Germans found the first trenches empty. When they had recovered from this surprise, they came up against the "suicide squads," which they thought to be the main defenders. As these troops fought desperately against the overwhelming odds and then retreated—those still alive—the Germans came on to meet the long-range rifle and machine gun fire of the real Allied forces. Said the Rainbow's history:

Despite repeated courageous attempts during which here and there some Germans got into the infantry position, they were stopped—stopped dead.

The Germans, the twenty-five divisions that had attacked, retreated, and the Allies were able to take the initiative and the offensive for the first time on the Western Front.

"Paris," said MacArthur, "could breathe again." He had personally directed the artillery fire of his brigade as it met the attack, and had been with his men in the trenches. General Gouraud cited the Rainbow Division, and MacArthur received his second Silver Star for gallantry in action.

A few days later, instead of getting an expected rest, the Rainbow Division was ordered to the Château-Thierry sector, to relieve the American 26th Division, which had suffered some five thousand casualties.

Under the pressure of French and American counterattacks, the Germans were moving out, the first few miles of their bitter retreat to the German border. But the withdrawal was orderly and desperately fought from stone wall to stone wall, town to own, farm building to farm building. Facing the deadly crossfire of mortars and machine guns, MacArthur remembered the Indian fighting of his youth and deployed his men in pairs and threes against the German strong points.

The Division fought its way forward in the now historic battles of La Croix Rouge Ferme, Beuvardes, Fôret de Fère and Villers-sur Fère, until they reached the south bank of the Ourcq River. The Rainbow crossed it on July 28, took the village of Meurcy Ferme in a vicious bayonet charge, then stormed the little town of Sergy, taking it and losing it eleven times before gaining permanent possession. The last town in that advance, Seringes et Nesles, fell before an attack which MacArthur personally led. The garrison died to a man in its defense, and MacArthur was cited for his third Silver Star.

Sensing that the Germans were withdrawing still farther, MacArthur undertook a personal reconnaissance, found his hunch to be true, and made his way back to headquarters to so report. Without rest for four days, he fell asleep almost before he had finished talking. Taking advantage of the conditions, MacArthur stated, his division was able to advance its artillery and infantry against little or no resistance. He was cited for his fourth Silver Star.

MacArthur's report of the reconnaissance notes that it had brought him in conjunction with the 165th New York, and its First Battalion commander, medal of honor winner Major William T. Donovan, known then and later as "Wild Bill" Donovan. To his World War I reputation, this fine soldier added more laurels in World War II as General "Wild Bill" Donovan, organizer of the OSS (Office of Strategic Services).

The Fighting Douglas MacArthur at Wake Island, wearing his insignia as a Five-Star General and the Distinguished Service Medal.

RECORD OF MacARTHUR'S BAPTISM HERE

From the Arkansas Gazette
March 18 1942

Baptisms
Communicants. 236 June 16/99

DAY.	DATE. No.	NAMES.	C.R.	Whence Received.	Education
May 16	1886	Malcolm McArthur		Born at New Orleans, La. 17th October A.D. 1876	
		Douglas McArthur		Little Rock, Ark. Jan'y 26th 1880	

Parent: Arthur McArthur Jr. U.S.A. Mrs. Mary Pinkney MacArthur Sponsor: Dr. A. L. Breysacher Miss Cornelia Busted " Emily Hardy

Parent: Arthur MacArthur Jr. U.S.A. Mrs. Mary Pinkney MacArthur Sponsor: Dr. Edwin Bentle Mrs. Ella Bentle

Baptismal record of Douglas MacArthur and his brother,
Malcolm, dated May 16, 1880, in Little Rock, Arkansas.

In this old arsenal building, now part of MacArthur City Park,
Little Rock, Arkansas, Douglas MacArthur was born.

Class portrait of Douglas MacArthur, West Point cadet class of 1903.

MacArthur receives the Distinguished Service Medal from General John J. Pershing, March 16, 1919, one of the few times he ever wore the military "tin hat" and then only because Pershing ordered him to do so.

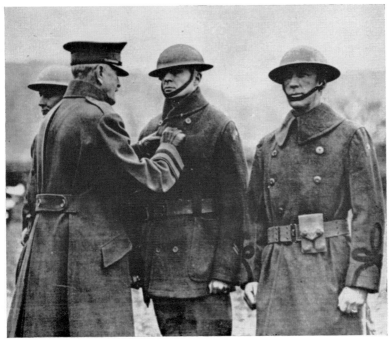

As a Four-Star General, Mac-Arthur is pictured here after taking the oath of office as Army Chief of Staff, December, 1930.

Mrs. Douglas MacArthur and their son, Arthur, in 1943, after their escape to Australia.

Manila welcomes MacArthur as military advisor in 1935. Behind him, with the straw hat, is then Colonel Dwight D. Eisenhower.

MacArthur with Major General Jonathan Wainwright, during Philippine field maneuvers in October, 1941, shortly before Pearl Harbor.

MacArthur on Corregidor, in March, 1942, with Major General Richard Sutherland.

Visiting a military hospital in Queensland, Australia, MacArthur talks to Private First Class Rosir Skinner of Adrian, Georgia, November, 1943.

On the bridge of the USS *Phoenix*, February 29, 1944, MacArthur watches the bombardment of Los Negros Island, one of the Admiralties, preparatory to landing. Notice the ear plugs to protect against the blast of heavy guns. With MacArthur are Colonel Lloyd Lehrbas and Rear Admiral Berkey.

After wading ashore, MacArthur strides down a path off the beach at Moratai Island, one of the Halmahera Group, September 15, 1944. Next stop: the Philippines. With him is aide, Colonel Larry Lehrbas.

MacArthur wades ashore at Leyte, to make his famous "I will return" speech.

Riding in a jeep, MacArthur inspects ruined town of Leyte.

On Christmas Day, 1944, MacArthur and the Philippines' President Sergio Osmena leave the newly established capital at Tacloban on Leyte Island.

At Camp O'Donnell, on Luzon Island, where the infamous "death march" of Bataan prisoners ended, MacArthur inspects dog tag on a cross.

MacArthur's first night in Yokohama is marked by a reunion with his old friend, General Wainwright, just released from a Japanese prison camp. At left is Lieutenant General Sir Arthur Percival, British commander at Singapore, also just released.

MacArthur signs the Japanese surrender document aboard the USS *Missouri,* August 31, 1945. Behind him are Generals Wainwright and Percival.

With Admiral Halsey, left, and General Eichelberger, General MacArthur salutes the first American flag raised over the American Embassy in Tokyo since Pearl Harbor.

General MacArthur receives Emperor Hirohito in Tokyo.

Admiral Lord Louis Mounbatten, Supreme Allied Commander, Southeast Asia Theater, visits General MacArthur in Manila.

MacArthur's famous C-54, the *Bataan*.

General MacArthur with Mrs. MacArthur at the Manila independence ceremonies.

MacArthur with President Syngman Rhee at South Korean independence ceremonies, August 15, 1948.

General MacArthur speaks before the San Francisco City Hall after a half million Americans had welcomed him back to his home shores. Mrs. MacArthur is at right of picture.

The General Douglas Mac-
Arthur Memorial Building in
Norfolk, Virginia.

MacArthur statue at Inchon,
Korea, where he made the
landing which saved the nation and an American Army.

Douglas MacArthur makes his famous address to a joint session of Congress on April 19, 1951, during which he quoted from a barracks ballad the moving and significant words, "Old soldiers never die. They just fade away."

In the Rainbow's history, Major Donovan related his own story of the crossing of the Ourcq, in a sector just adjacent to MacArthur's attack. He said:

The next morning [July 29] we were ordered to connect up with the Ohio Regiment on our left and advance to a new objective. The machine gunners had climbed in so close to us in the night that it was very difficult to move. . . . To get our position we had to move up the flank and had to face a machine gun nest with two machine guns and they put forth a burst of fire as each man crossed the open space. The first ten men crossing dropped, shot, and yet the next, without a flutter, went over. There were some fine examples of daring and courage.

Finally we got back where the stream took a bend and we were able to get under cover of a bank. I had found that most of our troops in advancing had taken the formation from the books. They had forgotten that these formations were made to advance with protection of artillery fire. I insisted that Company Commanders send their men forward as we used to do in the olden days, which is two or three at a time, moving fast and when they have advanced a few yards—flop. This gives the machine gunners a small target to fire at.

Then, covering this advance, I had our machine gunners open in the general direction of where I heard the Boche machine gun fire and then put with each machine gun, snipers to pick off the Boche personnel. With that system working, we went up the valley.

It was more difficult on the hill slopes because we had to charge machine gun nests with resultant losses. One sergeant took a platoon against a machine gun nest. He had twenty men when he started and when he reached the gun he had four. But he took the gun and the seven men who were serving it. We took very few prisoners. . . .

Several officers and men were wounded and killed, and when I heard that Captain Bootz who was just ahead of me was wounded, I ran forward to see that the line was steadied. I met him as he was being carried out and lay down by the side of the stream to talk to him.

Ames [one of Donovan's men] came running up behind to look out for me. I ordered him back, but he just smiled and said he was going to stay with me.

He came up and lay beside me. A sniper began to play on us, and machine bullets whizzed over our heads. I half turned and as I did, a sniper's bullet crossed my shoulder and struck Ames in the ear. He died instantly.

I reached for him and as I did another bullet struck me in the hand. I rolled into the creek, worked my way up to a group of men and with the fire playing over us, stayed there for three quarters of an hour in mud and water up above our waists. Later . . . I got the men out and into a wood Bois Colas, which was in the very center of the position, and dug in for the night.

All that night we held on and all the next day, with no food, the machine guns sweeping us constantly. The next day just on a poker hunch I started a little attack myself against a trench the Germans had, and as luck would have it, found that they had a group of twenty-five men just ready to rush our machine gun position. Out of the twenty-five I was able to save only two prisoners.

We had a hard time that afternoon. I had left my place to lead a skirmish line. By the way, I had been previously hit on the chest with a piece of stone or shell which ripped my gas mask and another piece of shell had hit me on the left heel tearing my shoe and throwing me off balance, while somehow I got some shrapnel in my leg. I guess I have been born to be hanged.

All my headquarters officers had been killed or wounded except Weller. I had Joyce Kilmer, who was a Sergeant and a poet, acting as my Sergeant Major, my own Sergeant Major having been wounded. Kilmer got a bullet in his head; we have buried him beside Ames.

(MacArthur's report also mentions Kilmer's death, noting that he was buried beside one of the trees he loved so much.)

Although he had been a Brigadier on June 26, MacArthur was not given command of the 84th Brigade until after the Château-Thierry drive. The staff he had directed in assembling, training and leading the Rainbow Division gave him, on parting, a silver cigarette box engraved: "To the bravest of the brave."

The division had lost nearly half its effective combat personnel in the vicious battles of the Ourcq and now was withdrawn for a rest during the month of August and to train thousands of replacements. This, with MacArthur, was a personal thing and he spent many hours checking and rechecking the effectiveness of blending the new green soldiers with the veterans of the 84th. Then in September, the Rainbow was ordered back into the lines as part of the Fourth American Army Corps (Pershing had his dream at last: an American Army) for the attack of San Mihiel.

The Germans had driven the deep San Mihiel salient into the French lines in 1914 and had held it against repeated attacks since. Thrusting across the Meuse River, blocking communications and movement between Paris and Verdun, it was highly valuable to the Germans, highly dangerous to the Allies. It was now to be the target for a massive French and American drive.

Positioned in the center, the Rainbow jumped off at 5:00 A.M., on September 12. With MacArthur directing, the 84th Brigade struck at the German flank, advanced farther than any other unit and took ten thousand prisoners. MacArthur was cited with his fifth Silver Star. His report on the second day read:

The morning of the second day's attack we not only reached but passed the army objective. I am sorry to say we just missed capturing the headquarters of the 19th Army Corps in the St. Benoit Chateau. Amongst many other evidences of their hasty departure we found a fully-set dining room table and a prepared meal.

From the cupola of the chateau which until the Germans destroyed it by shell fire was a favorite observation post, for the higher ranking officers of the division, to say nothing of visitors from the corps headquarters, I could see the dust of the German trains retreating down the roads toward Metz. Prisoners captured insisted that there was only a small garrison in Metz—nothing like the large numbers needed to really garrison and hold its defenses.

That night, General MacArthur, with his adjutant, made one of his famous personal reconnaissances into the outskirts of the city and discovered, as he had suspected, that it was practically undefended.

He returned and pleaded, first that the Rainbow Division and then that his 84th Brigade be allowed to march on the great prize city of Metz that night. He promised to occupy the city hall by daylight.

His plea was denied. There were other war plans and, within a week, the Germans had poured thousands of reinforcements to this key point in the Hindenburg Line and it was again impregnable. On September 25, MacArthur was ordered to stage a diversionary attack on the city, while the main battle line was being mounted in the Meuse-Argonne. Leading his Brigade, MacArthur cleared his advance with a tremendous artillery barrage and then maneuvered his forces skillfully just out of gunfire, creating the desired effect with the loss of only twenty men killed and wounded. He was cited for his sixth Silver Star.

October, 1918, saw the Rainbow Division moving through the cold rain of an early autumn into the Meuse-Argonne, where an army of a million Americans had started the drive which ended the war. As with San Mihiel, the Germans had taken the Argonne in 1914 and had never been dislodged. In

October, the Rainbow went into the trenches at Exermont, facing the Côte de Chatillon, which had repeatedly repulsed attacks. Colonel Hughes, who replaced MacArthur as Chief of Staff of the Rainbow, explained the position at the time, as recorded in official history:

A careful study of the situation (gained partly from another personal reconnaissance of MacArthur) showed that the Côte de Chatillon was the key to the whole situation, not only because of its physical characteristics and the position which it occupied, but also because it was very strongly held by the Germans, who apparently after our first attacks had increased its garrison.

When there could no longer be any doubt that only by the capture of the Côte de Chatillon, the apex of the German position paralleling the salient which the Rainbow had taken over, could our drive succeed, MacArthur asked permission to concentrate on the Côte de Chatillon and that the 151st Minnesota Field Artillery be placed directly under his command for the attack.

General Menoher held a conference at the Division command post after which he, MacArthur and I went to see General Summerall, the Corps Commander. From there we went to General Drum, the Chief of Staff of the 1st Army.

Both Summerall and General Drum said that MacArthur could not capture the Côte de Chatillon with his Brigade alone. However, they finally yielded to our arguments and MacArthur was given permission to go ahead.

Consequently, MacArthur, as had happened before in his life and would happen again, found himself in the dramatic position where his own personal military achievement would influence history. Not only the leaders of the American officers present at the moment, but military historians since are practically unanimous in their agreement that this one point, the Côte de Chatillon, was the key not only to the highly fortified Kriemhilde Stellung, which stretched across that sector, but to the entire Argonne offensive—and to victory in World War I.

MacArthur's own report of the battle reads, in part:

When the orders first came for the attack on the Division and I looked at the map and saw the ground in front of the 84th Infantry Brigade and then followed this with a personal reconnaissance, I had many misgivings.

He continues, citing the many attacks which had failed:

This was so much the case that when General Menoher asked me whether or not I could take the Côte de Chatillon I could not help telling him as long as we were speaking in the strictest confidence that I was not certain. I gave him the reasons why.

But, when General Summerall came around the night before the attack and asked the same question, I replied: "General Summerall, this brigade assures you that it will capture Côte de Chatillon. If this brigade does not capture Chatillon, you can publish a casualty list of the entire brigade with the brigade commander's name at the top."

Tears sprang into General Summerall's eyes. He was evidently so moved he could say nothing. He looked at me for a few seconds and then left without a word.

MacArthur had long ago fathomed the weakness of the German military leaders on defense. He kept his center strong, but his flanks were frequently only weakly covered. It may have been inherent in the German character that he both attacked and expected attack, head-on.

So, for this strike MacArthur sent his Iowa regiment to the left side and his Alabama regiment to the right in a pincer movement to envelop the strong point. Critical to the success of the movement was his discovery, through an airplane reconnaissance photo, of a break in the barbed wire defenses at the right.

For the three days and nights of October 14, 15 and 16, the men of the two regiments, MacArthur with them, fought through the rain and mud, from one bit of cover to another, from one bit of danger to another. Wrote MacArthur:

Death, cold and remorseless, whistled and sang its way through our ranks.

A note from the Rainbow's history, written by Lieutenant Colonel Walter E. Bare of the Alabama Regiment, reads:

Late that night General MacArthur came by . . . on an inspection tour. While we were talking the Germans were constantly shelling the valley with gas shells, mostly mustard and tear gas. I remember well that both the General and I consumed so much of the gas we could hardly see or talk.

At the end of the three days, MacArthur's 84th Brigade held the Côte de Chatillon. The Kriemhilde Stellung, the last German fortification across the Argonne, had been broken.

(*Stellung* translates into a strong or heavily fortified line of defense. *Kriemhilde,* in German folklore and Wagnerian opera [and in the *Niebelungen*], was the wife of *Siegfried,* legendary German hero, slayer of dragons and consort of the *valkyries.* The Germans had another and greater defense *stellung,* the *Siegfried Line,* which did not prove invincible, either.)

Many citations and many honors went to the men of the Brigade. General Menoher, the Rainbow Division commander, recommended MacArthur both for promotion to major general and for the Medal of Honor. The recommendation (to General Pershing) for promotion read:

For his field leadership, generalcy and determination during three days of constant combat in front of the Côte de Chatillon,

I am happy to recommend to you for a second time that he be made a major general.

The recommendation went up the line. General Summerall concurred, as did General Pershing, sending it on to the Secretary of War. Baker also approved, terming MacArthur "the greatest front line general of the war." As noted previously, the war ended and all promotions were frozen before MacArthur could receive his second star. The awards board did not concur in the recommendation for the Medal of Honor, awarding him a second Distinguished Service Cross instead.

The early days of November saw a beaten German army suing for peace and in full retreat, but fighting every inch of the way as it gave ground. The Rainbow was assigned to the First Corps, which had orders to drive straight for the city of Sedan. The 84th took off and in a report MacArthur wrote:

Drove the brigade hard all the night of the fifth and cleared the forest. Received a sniper's bullet through the sleeve of my coat. Close shave but it did not even scratch me. These Germans never give up.

MacArthur won his seventh Silver Star for this drive to the gates of Sedan, although the French were accorded the honor of making the actual entry. And, on November 6, MacArthur was given command of the Rainbow Division. General Monoher, who moved up to the command of a Corps, noted in his farewell to the Rainbow that "MacArthur has actually commanded larger bodies of troops on the battleline than any other officer in our Army, with, in each instance, conspicuous success."

He also noted that MacArthur, although twice wounded, in more than a year had spent no day apart from his command.

At the change-of-command ceremonies, General Pershing personally decorated him with the Distinguished Service Medal and it was one of the few times MacArthur ever wore a helmet—on Pershing's orders.

November 11 saw the Armistice, and General MacArthur became part of the Army of Occupation in Germany. Then, and only then, did he permit himself the luxury of falling ill with a culmination of the various throat infections from which he had suffered throughout the war. He lay dangerously close to death for ten days before recovering.

April of 1919 saw him sailing homeward with the last units of the Rainbow Division. Of the forty thousand men who had served with it, two thousand seven hundred and fifteen were listed dead and thirteen thousand two hundred and eighty wounded. Most remarkably, the Rainbow lost only forty-one in prisoners—a tremendous tribute to remarkable leadership.

8

☆ ☆ ☆ ☆ ☆

SAFELY BACK from the battlefields of World War I, thirty-nine years old and about to be made the youngest brigadier general in the Regular Army by an Act of Congress, Douglas MacArthur was appointed Superintendent of the United States Military Academy.

In giving him the assignment, Chief of Staff, General Peyton C. March, said "West Point is forty years behind the times."

He could have added much more. The need for officers during the war just past had been so great (more than two thousand officers had been killed or died of wounds during its course) that the Academy courses had been shortened to three, then two, and finally to one year. The previous November, just ten days before the Armistice, had seen the two classes graduated, leaving only the plebes.

Even worse, the general attitude of both the public and Congress was that, since the nation had just finished a war to end all wars, why should a military academy be necessary?

MacArthur had first to win support in the right Congressional Committees, which he did persuasively and successfully, and then to rebuild the Academy curriculum, training and esprit in the image of the twentieth century, and not the nineteenth.

His assault upon the heretofore sacrosanct prerogatives—autonomy and inflexible petrifaction of the Old Guard faculty—provided a reasonable example of the irresistible force meeting the immovable object. The previous superintendent had been seventy-one years old on retirement and he had ascended to the position, like other superintendents, after years as a professor. This fellow, this mere stripling, fresh from the trenches of France, could presume to revise the scholastic courses and the teaching methods which had produced the Lees and the Grants—and even MacArthur himself?

It was a monumental struggle—and MacArthur won. When possible, he used indirection and tactical suggestions. He won bits of ground with flank attacks. When necessary, however, he overwhelmed his stubbornly entrenched antagonists by surprise frontal attacks.

For generations, cadets had gone into "summer camp" on the Academy grounds. There, from neat rows of orderly tents stretched along immaculate company fronts, the future officers had drilled in the morning, "suffered" through leisurely afternoons and evenings, sometimes strolling with their dates, dancing at formal and informal "hops" or in pleasant conversation. Their meals were served in mess halls with civilian waiters. White-clad sentries walked proscribed posts in the moonlight, calling out the traditional "Who goes there?" at any approach.

Watching all this from the immediate background of two years in the trenches and barbed wire of France, where the enemy fired at anything that moved, MacArthur shook his head in wonder. He wondered, too, why he had not thought it unrealistic as a cadet.

Then he ordered the summer camp bulldozed into an

athletic field and made arrangements with Washington head-quarters to have all three classes (except plebes) attached for the summer to one of the regular divisions for the rugged field training and war games the pros went through.

He observed the harsh, biting language used by the upperclassmen in handling plebes and wondered if this might be the only method of handling men that these future officers would know when they graduated and had to work with troops. A little investigation revealed that many of the young West Point lieutenants had to be taught later—sometimes by their experienced noncoms—that the "new army" didn't respond to the savage dressing down, the curt sarcasm and the brutal tongue lashing. MacArthur knew, as the cadets didn't, that many an American officer had been shot in the back by his own men for just such treatment in the "civilian army" of World War I.

So the Superintendent put regular officers in charge of the West Point plebes, with orders to treat them as soldiers and not "beasts." He abolished the remaining remnants of the hazing system, while still leaving the traditional respect due the upperclassmen. They must always be addressed as "Sir" or "Mister." They were allowed to "brace" to plebes and the barrier of no social contact was maintained, for the plebe must always know that he is unproven and on trial.

With the upperclassmen gone through early graduation, the honor system had fallen by the wayside. Obviously it was needed, but you couldnt regulate a cadet to "be honest." MacArthur named a group of responsible and thoughtful cadets into an Honor Committee, to re-establish some of the old "Thou must nots"—cheating, lying and conduct generally unbecoming an officer and a gentleman. His method worked.

He felt that the old system, wherein cadets never handled money but used chits (and their dates always paid their own way), plus the fact that they seldom got off the Academy grounds, gave them an overly sheltered concept of the world they must enter. He started the custom of week-end passes ("even the lowliest recruit gets that much") and restored money to circulation.

Detesting unnecessary "paper work" himself, MacArthur abolished the system whereby cadets replied to "skins" by endorsement. They reported orally to their tactical officers instead, much as their own men would report to them later, as troop commanders.

The Superintendent horrified the professors and instructors by visiting their classes and actually asking questions! He scoured the Army for officers who had had modern experience in teaching (as opposed to being simply West Pointers) and gently crammed them down the throats of department heads, who choked visibly at the idea, let alone the fact that an officer from the wrong side of the tracks should be teaching West Point cadets! He gradually revised the curriculum, to place more emphasis on such studies as history, English and the humanities.

He refused to permit faculty department heads to dismiss their subordinate teachers without good reason, suspecting clashes in personality—or perhaps, at times, clashes in the personalities of the wives involved. Similarly, he questioned closely the requests for new teachers by name, delving into the qualifications of the officers in question. West Point was a "cushy" post and it was always pleasant to have friends about.

During his years at the Academy, General MacArthur established the working schedule he was to follow the rest of his life. His mother, of course, had moved into the Superintendent's quarters with him and functioned graciously as his hostess. He would arrive at his office punctually at eleven and spend an hour with his adjutant (only MacArthur called him his chief of staff) and other subordinates. The hour between twelve and one was given over to interviews. He returned to his quarters for lunch, one to three, and then usually spent the remainder of the day, except for committee or staff meetings, observing and checking the cadet activities.

The concentration of studies and the early graduations during the war had virtually abolished the Academy's athletic program, and one of MacArthur's first actions was to restore it. He instituted massive intramural competition, with every cadet participating in every sport, and then began to build the varsity teams which would compete with other schools, notably, of course, the Naval Academy.

Douglas MacArthur had found during the war, he said, that men accustomed to winning acquired the habit. Since there was no substitution for victory in war, it was good to acquire the habit before the fighting started, and he wanted his cadets versed in the custom.

Furthermore, he had found that good athletes also made good officers. He caused to have carved on the stone portals of the Cadet gymnasium these words of his own belief:

> Upon the fields of friendly strife
> are sown the seeds
> that upon other fields in other days,
> will bear the fruits of victory.

If there had been active recruiting of athletic material into the ranks of West Point cadets, it had been kept very quiet. MacArthur made no bones about his own feelings in this matter. He set his coaches and their assistants to scouring the high-school grounds and campuses of the nation in search of men who could pass a football, pitch a no-hitter or run the hundred in less than ten seconds—and still qualify in the brains department. One officer remarked later that he spent so much time in the Pennsylvania coal country that he felt he should have had a union card.

The criticism which followed his search for athletes slid lightly from Mac's shoulders as he watched the West Point teams acquire the prowess they needed for successful competition. The night after West Point won its first major victory over Annapolis (in baseball) the cadets staged an after-hours pajama parade that wound through the Academy grounds for some time.

The next day, MacArthur was chatting with the commandant of cadets.

"That was quite an affair we had last night," he remarked. The commandant, an Army colonel, agreed.

"How many did you 'skin'?" MacArthur asked.

"Not a darned one," replied the colonel. "In fact, I went out and made a little victory speech to them."

"I know you did," said Mac. "And I was tempted to join you."

MacArthur's training in public relations with the General Staff prior to World War I found a reflection many times during his tour of duty as Superintendent at West Point. There were frequent visits of dignitaries and personages, both American and foreign, and Douglas MacArthur tried always to break from the deadly dull formalities of the past.

When the Prince of Wales (now the Duke of Windsor), who was then of college age, paid a visit to the Point, MacArthur got him through the early ceremonies and then His Highness found himself in the company of four cadets of his own age. They strolled around the grounds for more than an hour, free of the normal royal entourage and returned laughing and chatting with easy and youthful informality. The Prince wrote a grateful letter of appreciation.

Each visiting Congressman found himself with a cadet "aide" from his own state, who could talk of local interests and who tried to anticipate any personal needs during the visit. When a group of French cadets arrived, MacArthur detailed a French-speaking West Pointer to each and they were given an easy, informal freedom of the barracks and grounds.

Douglas MacArthur was not, in the normal sense of the word, a socially inclined man. He could dance, as all West Point cadets are required to learn to dance, but it was more a duty to him than a pleasure. He was widely and well read and a thoughtful man who could discourse intelligently and interestingly on many subjects, but he had neither talent nor liking for small talk. Prohibition was in effect during his duty tour at West Point, of course, but he drank little either before or later. (At parties he would usually ask for a gimlet, a favorite drink of the English in the Far East, and then nurse it through the evening. It gave him something to hold and prevented anxious hostesses from pressing other drinks upon him.)

He and his mother rarely entertained informally at the Academy, although they, of course, attended the normal functions of both cadets and faculty during the years there.

It was at a West Point ball that MacArthur met and fell in love with the girl who was to be his first wife, the socialite-divorcee and heiress, Mrs. Henrietta Louise Cromwell Brooks. MacArthur proposed to her the night they met and if she didn't accept on the spot, her answer was certainly far from a refusal.

If the handsome MacArthur, youngest brigadier in the Army, was considered quite a catch, Mrs. Cromwell Brooks was more than eligible herself. Her first husband had been Walter D. Brooks, Jr., a Baltimore business and social leader, by whom she bore two children and from whom she collected a substantial settlement on separation. Her father, Oliver Cromwell, had left the family more than well off financially and her mother had subsequently married E. T. Stotesbury, a banker reputedly worth $150,000,000. Her brother, Jimmy Cromwell, was later the first husband of Doris Duke, the tobacco heiress.

In courting and marrying Louise Cromwell Brooks, Douglas MacArthur demonstrated more of the reckless courage and disregard of danger which had made him one of the most decorated officers in the Army. At the time of his proposal and virtual acceptance, Mrs. Brooks was understood to be unofficially engaged to General John J. "Black Jack" Pershing, Chief of Staff and MacArthur's boss, who was some thirty years older than the girl. She was also being courted rather hesitantly by a colonel on Pershing's immediate staff.

Mrs. Brooks had met General Pershing in Paris, where she divorced her first husband. In the early postwar days, the commander of the American forces entertained her and her brother frequently, in his sumptuous Paris quarters, along with the military and diplomatic figures of the time. When Pershing returned to Washington, Mrs. Brooks found it convenient to come also. In Washington, she became General Pershing's official hostess.

When Mrs. Brooks broke the news of her attachment to MacArthur to Pershing, the Army Chief of Staff reportedly told her, "You may not like him so well in the Philippines." She didn't.

The marriage took place at *El Mirasol*, a Palm Beach villa owned by the bride's mother, on February 22, 1922, and the couple walked to the altar along a path decorated with red, white and blue banners and the flags of West Point and the Rainbow Division. The bride wore chiffon, apricot in color, and a diamond necklace, the gift of the groom. General Mac-

Arthur wore his Army dress whites, heavily hung with the medals he had won. After a honeymoon in Florida, they returned to West Point to set up housekeeping in the Superintendent's quarters. The senior Mrs. MacArthur, who had encouraged her son in the courtship and marriage, moved out.

Three months later, and nearly a year before his normal tour would have been up, MacArthur was assigned to the Philippines.

Said the bride, "Jack wanted me to marry him. When I wouldn't, he wanted me to marry one of his colonels. I wouldn't do that either, so here I am—packing for the Philippines."

As predicted, the new Mrs. MacArthur was not happy in the Islands. She found the life there boring and she learned that her husband's preoccupation with his career made him impatient with the gayer life she liked. The discordant notes first struck in Manila remained in the air on the couple's return to the United States and after MacArthur had been promoted to major general—with some help, perhaps, from her family. The pair were divorced in Reno in 1928.

Mrs. MacArthur married twice more, MacArthur once—some fifteen years later. From her home in Washington's Georgetown, where she was suffering from chronic bronchial pneumonia, his first wife prepared a statement for the press when Douglas MacArthur died. When no call for this came, she telephoned it to a newspaper, but later told this writer,

"I do not want to talk to anyone about General Douglas MacArthur ever."

For his part, MacArthur mentioned his first marriage briefly in his memoirs and omitted it entirely from his *Who's Who* biography.

9

WHILE Major General MacArthur was still in his corps command at Baltimore, he was named to serve in one of the most unpleasant assignments of his military career—the historic court-martial of his old and close friend, Brigadier General Billy Mitchell.

When General Mitchell was tried on charges of insubordination, the basis of the sensational trial was the role of air power in the American military system.

Billy Mitchell had been one of the most brilliant of American air commanders in World War I, as well as a distinguished combat flyer. Returning from the battlefields of France, he took up the leadership of the small band of Army flyers dedicated to the belief that air power would be a predominant factor in any future war. Mitchell challenged the Navy's traditional role as the nation's first line of defense. He marshaled strong congressional opinion behind his ideas. He organized a demonstration which proved that aerial bombs could sink any naval craft from a submarine to a battleship. He fought to get money to develop bombardment and fighter aircraft. He wanted an air arm separate from the Army. He antagonized almost every "old-line" general and admiral in the service.

While his superiors suggested pointedly that his campaign was verging on insubordination (much as MacArthur's had ten years earlier in the matter of mobilizing the National Guard for service in France), General Mitchell set out deliberately to provoke a hearing that would carry his fight to the public. He accomplished his goal in September, 1925, when the Navy's big dirigible, the *Shenandoah,* bound for exhibitions at state fairs, broke up in a storm. The commander and thirteen members of the crew were killed. Mitchell, who had no faith or belief in dirigibles or other lighter-than-air craft, charged that the accident was the result of "incompetency, criminal negligence and almost treasonable administration of the national defense by the War and Navy Departments." The charge and trial by court-martial followed.

The trial was doubly distasteful to MacArthur. He agreed, in some degree, with Mitchell about the value of air power, but, although he had always championed the right of military men to speak out for the causes in which they believed, at the same time, he deplored the intemperance of Mitchell's statements. More, Billy Mitchell was a long-time and close personal friend.

The Mitchells, like the MacArthurs, were from Milwaukee. The grandfathers of Billy and Douglas had been friends one hundreds years before. In the Civil War, their fathers had fought in the same Wisconsin regiment. Young Billy (four years older than Douglas) had served as a lieutenant under General Arthur MacArthur in the Philippines. Douglas had courted Billy's sisters, Janet and Harriet. Douglas had invited Billy to speak at West Point when he was Commandant. Billy and his bride, on their honeymoon, had visited Douglas and *his* bride in Manila.

The trial lasted seven weeks and the defense counsel, Representative Reid of Pennsylvania, adroitly turned the tenor of it away from the insubordination of Mitchell to a presentation of a case for military air power. The witnesses who testified or were present made a list of the Air Force leaders of the next generation and the next war—Hap Arnold, Tooey Spaatz, Ira Eaker, Jimmy Doolittle, George Kenney and others.

Major General Douglas MacArthur took his place at the trial table, after greeting General Mitchell warmly when he entered the room, then listened without speaking for the duration of the hearing.

At the close and after deliberating three hours, the court found Mitchell guilty, suspending him from rank, command and duty, with forfeiture of all pay and allowances, for five years. When the sentence was announced, MacArthur sat, still silent, his face narrowed and drawn. Even Mitchell noticed it, with the remark that, "MacArthur looks as though he had been drawn through a knothole."

Choosing to keep his own counsel, according to the protocol of such affairs, MacArthur suffered many indictments throughout the years as having joined in the "persecution" of Mitchell, and as being a party to the reactionary officers who drove him from the service. It was not until MacArthur himself left the service, more than twenty years later, that he revealed he had cast the one "not guilty" ballot on the verdict—and had saved Mitchell from outright dismissal from the Army. The two men remained friends until Mitchell's death in 1936.

Three years after Mitchell's trial, MacArthur found another break in his peacetime military service more pleasantly diverting. Due, perhaps, to his emphasis on athletics while Commandant at West Point and to his enthusiasm for the physical fitness of his troops, he was named President of the

American Olympic Committee for the 1928 summer games in
Amsterdam.

It was a job he liked and took seriously (although some of
the stories about his direction of the team may be apocryphal,
for example: that he ordered one winded and protesting
athlete, who had just won the 400 meters, to run again in the
1,600-meter relay race "because your country needs you."

Sectional trials were held for the American Olympic athletes, culminating in finals at Harvard stadium on July 6 and
7, 1928. The team left for Holland on the chartered S.S.
Roosevelt, July 11, with one hundred and one athletes on the
track and field team, including nineteen women who were
competing in these events for the first time. Along with
boxers, wrestlers, oarsmen, fencers, coaches, trainers, friends
and relatives, the total passenger list was two hundred and
fifty-eight persons, including MacArthur. Accounts of the day
show it to have been a peaceful voyage in every way, and
the ship docked in good order. It was used as a floating hotel
for the team, a circumstance which later was blamed for the
lack of tiptop condition in some of the contestants.

The games opened on July 28, with 40,000 persons in the
stands and, according to the news accounts, some 75,000
more milling around the gates, trying to get in. The French
team, refused admission by a confused (and militant) gate-
keeper, lodged an official protest and an international incident was narrowly averted. The Finns, unable to get up
to the gate, were more resourceful; they crawled over the
wall, en masse.

Prince Hendrik of Holland, acting for Queen Wilhelmina,
took the salutes of the parading national delegations and ac-
knowledged the dipped flags of all forty-three nations save
two. The French missed the parade, due to the altercation at
the gates, and the United States, as MacArthur reminded his

athletes, does not dip its flag to foreign rulers. America's color bearer, shot-putter Bud Houser, who won his event the next day, thereupon marched by the Prince with his standard held high.

The American team won first place in the track and field events, always considered the major factors in the Olympic Games, but to some American sports writers the victory was somewhat less than resounding. While the United States took eight first places, only three were in track events and two of these were relays. (Ray Barbuto won the only individual running event, the 400 meters, in the time of 47.8. The 1960 Olympic time, also American, was 44.9 seconds.) The other first came in the field events.

The sports writers pointed out that tiny Finland, with only a fraction of our population, had scored five firsts, all but one in the running events. This was in the days of the famous "flying Finns"—Paavo Nurmi, Larva, Ritola and Loukola.

Another "first" was recorded in these 1928 Olympics which probably had more significance for MacArthur than for any other spectator. Mikio Oda covered 49 feet, 10 and $^{13}\!/_{16}$ inches in the running hop, step and jump, to win Japan its first gold medal in any competition. Japan, the Olympic President must have noted, was truly emerging.

In one of the boxing contests which followed the track and field events, the American coaches protested a decision and threatened to withdraw the American team from competition. MacArthur overruled the coach in a widely publicized decision, saying sternly, "Americans are not quitters."

His report after the competition was equally MacArthurian, including these words:

"Nothing is more synonymous of our national success than is our national success in athletics. Nothing has been more characteristic of the genius of American people than their genius for athletics.

"The team proved itself a worthy successor of its brilliant predecessors."

His boss and Chief of Staff, General Summerall, wrote in turn:

"You have not only maintained the reputation that Americans do not quit, but that Americans know how to win."

Two years later, on November 21, 1930, Douglas MacArthur was sworn in as Chief of Staff of the Army and promoted to the four stars of a full general. He was fifty years old and thirty-one of those fifty had been spent in the military service. His immediate previous command had been two rather uneventful years in the Philippines, his third tour of duty there.

Writing about the Chief of Staff assignment many years later, MacArthur recalled that he shrank from what he felt would be a dreadful ordeal; that his mother, sensing his emotions, had cabled him to accept—and he did.

It is easy to believe that MacArthur, realizing quite well the low state of the Army at the time and the disinclination of the Congress to vote funds to improve it, felt that the assignment would be an ordeal.

It is not so easy to believe that he shrank from that ordeal. The office of Chief of Staff, highest military post in the Army (and probably the nation), had been his goal since the day he entered West Point—as he had so announced. He was a soldier with a soldier's discipline and the assignment to be Chief of Staff was an order from his Commander-in-Chief, President Hoover. Refusing it would have been unthinkable from a career point of view—or from almost any other point of view—for MacArthur. Such an action would have been completely out of the MacArthur character. He had never shrunk from ordeals or challenges; he welcomed them, whether it might be a combat patrol in the trenches or convincing an antagonist that the MacArthur way was the right way.

On accepting the assignment, he served with great distinction not only two full terms of two years each, but an extra year, at the request of another President, his old friend Franklin D. Roosevelt.

Much of MacArthur's effort during these five years was strenuously devoted to two parallel causes: first, to revitalize and modernize the American Army; second, to prevent the Congress from destroying it entirely. Like every other period in his career, this one was colorful, controversial and frequently dramatic. The American public has historically enjoyed worshiping the soldier in time of war and wishing he would go quietly away in time of peace. The conflict over, MacArthur, as the nation's top man in uniform, was denounced as a militarist and a "strutting popinjay." He was the target of every politician who sought votes in an economy-minded district. College students booed him as a "warmonger" when he advocated preparedness.

On one occasion he gathered up his papers and walked out of a Congressional committee hearing, saying, "Gentlemen, I have been insulted. I am as high in my profession as you are in yours. When you have apologized, I shall return." (The last three words reoccurred significantly some years later.)

When Congress threatened to cut the regular Army Officer Corps from 12,000 to 2,000, MacArthur told committeemen:

"An Army can live on short rations; it can be insufficiently clothed and housed; it can even be poorly armed. But in action it is doomed without the trained leadership of officers."

When the Bureau of the Budget, part of the Executive

Branch, got into the act and began slashing his requests for appropriations, MacArthur, with Secretary of War George H. Dern, called upon President Roosevelt. The General's arguments became so vehement that the President checked him sharply and angrily. Certain that his career was ended there and then, MacArthur offered his resignation. This was refused, and to the General's surprise, the cuts were restored. It is amazing, in the light of today's military budgets, to realize that the Army's expenditures in those days were: 1931—$335 million; 1933—$305 million; 1934—$277 million and 1935—$281 million.

In 1931, MacArthur visited France and saw the plans for the Maginot Line, which became the symbol of a static and disastrous defense. A year later, he visited Germany, where Hitler was just rising to power. Hermann Goering was advocating supremacy in the air as the key to military superiority and the German ground army leaders were projecting mobility and rapid maneuverability. General MacArthur returned impressed, suspecting, as he said, that the Germans would try again—as they did.

At home, his campaign to modernize the American Army reflected both his experience in World War I and his convictions that our preparations for the next war must keep pace with modern technology.

He established the Armored School at Fort Knox, which spawned the American armored divisions of World War II. He worked out an Industrial Mobilization Plan, which was the basis of that used for World War II, and the one in effect today.

He placed the army's air arm—the Army Air Corps—under the direct command of General Headquarters (GHQ) and established it as an independent striking force. Lack of funds stopped it far short of the one thousand planes he envisioned for it.

Equally important, he mechanized the ground troops of the Army, putting them on wheels and vastly increasing the fire power and effectiveness of the individual army unit. For the morale of both officer and enlisted man, he was instrumental in having designed and adopted a new uniform which gave them soft shirts, ties and lapels, instead of the age-old military blouse with its high, tight collar.

The most publicized and, as MacArthur has said, most poignant occurrence of his tenure as Chief of Staff was the affair of the Bonus March. Certainly it has been for many years the most misrepresented.

The year 1932 saw this country in the grip of its worst depression. Millions of men were out of work. Breadlines and soup kitchens were commonplace. President Hoover and Congress, the one Republican and the other Democratic, could or would find no solution.

In the spring of that year, an unemployed Oregon cannery employee with a gift of oratory and probably honest motives, started a hitchhiking movement of unemployed World War I veterans on Washington. The object of Walter W. Waters' movement was simple. He wanted Congress to amend a soldier's bonus law, voted in 1924, so as to permit the immediate cashing of bonus bonds—instead of waiting until 1944, when the bonds came due. Each man's share would have been about $1,000.

The vanguard reached Washington in May and, by early summer, the "Bonus Army" had grown to 20,000 men, women and children. At first they camped in partly demolished buildings on Pennsylvania Avenue. As the number grew, MacArthur ordered that Army tents be set up in the Anacostia Flats, outside the city, for this ragged, tattered mob.

He followed the tents with mobile Army kitchens and food until Congressional protests forced him to withdraw them.

By July, the situation had become explosive. The veterans had marched on the Capitol and to the White House, to be blocked and dispersed by police. There were charges, proven many years later, that the ranks of the "Bonus Army" had been infiltrated by both Communists and known criminals. At the time, these charges were dismissed, as they might be now, simply because it is common practice to tag any dissenter, particularly if he is troublesome, with an opprobrious term.

The chief of the Metropolitan police at the time was retired Brigadier General Pelham Glassford, a West Point schoolmate and friend of MacArthur's. The two men had discussed the situation many times, and Glassford had brought up the possibility of having to use Army troops at some point. MacArthur demurred strongly. Many of the "Bonus" marchers were from the Rainbow, his old division. Some of them he knew and had helped with his own money. Like the public generally, he was sympathetic.

Congress finally authorized payment of rail fares home for bona fide veterans, and many accepted. Instead of helping, this removed many of the honest and sincere leaders. Their successors, under whatever motive, encouraged the violence which broke out on July 28. In a clash with the District police, two veterans were killed. General Glassford was knocked down and mauled. The District commissioners requested federal troops.

The order, when it came to MacArthur, was from President Hoover via Secretary of War Patrick Hurley, and at MacArthur's insistence Hurley put it in writing, the pertinent part of which follows:

"You will have United States troops proceed immediately

to the scene of disorder. Cooperate fully with the District of Columbia police force which is now in charge. Surround the affected area and clear it without delay. Turn over all prisoners to the civil authorities. In your orders insist that any women and children who may be in the affected area be accorded every consideration and kindness. Use all humanity consistent with the due execution of this order."

From this point the controversy over MacArthur's part in the unhappy and mishandled—from the start—affair begins. Stories which were repeated, circulated, printed and believed (and probably still are) had MacArthur on a snow-white horse leading a charge against the ragged, shoeless (in many cases) and hungry veterans, firing into their ranks, killing many, burning their tents, destroying their meager possessions. In some stories he used tanks, in others bayonets. Furthermore, it was a task so much to his liking that he refused to delegate it to anyone else.

Factually, and the circumstances have been well established by a number of investigators throughout the years, the story is quite different.

MacArthur was in civilian attire when the order was received. He sent an orderly to his quarters at Fort Myer, where he lived with his mother, to return with a uniform. The uniform the orderly brought was the one MacArthur would normally have worn in the course of that or any other day. It had several rows of ribbons and the sharpshooter's medal which he prized.

MacArthur considered removing them but was deterred, he said later, by two thoughts: he had won them honestly; they might favorably impress some of the veterans who would recognize him.

MacArthur also considered delegating this unpleasant job to someone else, and it would have been the easiest of mat-

ters for the Chief of Staff to do so. He is recorded as saying,
"This job is the kiss of death for whoever carries it out. It
will ruin any man's career."

MacArthur was already Chief of Staff and could go no
higher in his military career. He probably wanted very much
to "let John do it" but would not.

The white horse simply didn't exist, or at least not that
day. With Brigadier General Perry Miles, the actual troop
commander, and two officers from the General Staff—Major
Dwight Eisenhower and Major George Patton—MacArthur
led six hundred troops to the "Bonus" march area on foot.

Using tear gas, and occasionally the flat side of sabers, the
troops advanced, driving the bonus marchers across the
Anacostia River. Not a shot was fired. There were no casualties and no injuries save for many a smarting eye. According to investigators, the marchers set fire to their own camp
site.

The autumn of 1935 found MacArthur completing his fifth
year as Chief of Staff, still comparatively young at fifty-five,
but with nowhere to go. The position of Corps Commander
was the next highest at that time and accepting it would have
meant stepping down from the rank of full general to the
two stars of a major general. In the business world it would
have been like giving up the presidency of a great corporation to become one of several vice presidents.

The problem, incidentally, of naming brilliant young officers to the top job and then wondering what to do with them
when the term is up, still exists. Today, however, there are
international assignments—General Eisenhower became Supreme Commander of the NATO forces at SHAPE after being Chief of Staff, for example—or even ambassadorships to
which top, retired service officers are assigned.

While he was considering what to do, MacArthur was approached by his old friend Manuel Quezon, shortly to be elected first President of the Philippine Commonwealth.

With the Philippines scheduled to be given their independence soon, Quezon was concerned with maintaining that independence. He asked MacArthur if he would become military advisor to the Commonwealth for the express purpose of building up its defenses. MacArthur accepted.

Two years later he retired, under some political pressure, and accepted the position of Field Marshal of the Philippine Forces. His mother had urged him to accept the Philippine assignment.

"It will lead to greater things," she told him. Her prophecy was correct. As related earlier, MacArthur was there and available for these greater things when World War II broke out.

10

☆ ☆ ☆ ☆ ☆

WHEN General Douglas MacArthur sailed for the Philippines aboard the S.S. *President Hoover* in October, 1935, he was accompanied by a small staff (including Major Dwight Eisenhower) and his aging mother, then eighty-two.

Mrs. MacArthur was suffering her last illness and she had insisted on going with her son, sensing that she would never see him again otherwise.

The night before the *President Hoover* docked in Honolulu, MacArthur attended a cocktail party on shipboard and there met the only other woman who would greatly influence his life—Jean Marie Faircloth of Murfreesboro, Tennessee.

Two months after her arrival in Manila, Douglas MacArthur's mother died. This was one of the saddest moments in his life. She had shared his interests and activities as no other person had. Mother and son were extraordinarily close. He was now alone. Both brothers, father and mother had died.

Fifteen months later, on April 30, 1937, after an unhurried courtship, he married Jean Faircloth in the New York Municipal Building. A city clerk officiated. It was one time in his life when Douglas MacArthur stepped out of character. Both courtship and wedding were remarkably undramatic.

Jean Faircloth was born on December 28, 1898, in Nashville, the daughter of Edward C. and Sallie Beard Faircloth. Later to become a prosperous banker and mill owner, Edward Faircloth was not so provident in the early days of his marriage and, not long after Jean's birth, her mother divorced her father and married Frederick Smith.

Jean grew up in Murfreesboro with her two brothers and a half brother and half sister. For a time, her mother turned the Beard family home into a summer hotel. In 1910, Mrs. Smith journeyed to New York and there played in summer stock under the name of Peggy Castleman. Returning to Murfreesboro, she found occupation easily, both acting and directing in the local Little Theater. Jean's stepfather had been an early suitor of her mother and when "Miss Sallie," as she was known in her home town, married Edward Faircloth, Frederick Smith left home, somewhat romantically, to tramp the foreign soil of a dozen countries in as many occupations, until Miss Sallie's divorce. Jean's own father was Canadian by birth. Having mended his ways, he accumulated a sizable fortune, part of which he used to finance Jean's schooling and travels. On his death, he left her an estate of some $200,000. Jean's grandfather, Confederate Captain Richard Beard, and Douglas MacArthur's father, Union Army Adjutant Arthur MacArthur, had fought on opposite sides in the Civil War battles of Missionary Ridge and Stones River.

Jean grew up in the Southern tradition of wide verandas, plenty of servants, and magnolia-scented moonlight. She was small of figure (five feet two inches, one hundred pounds), dark-haired and pretty. She inherited her mother's fondness for acting—and her mother's roles in the local stage plays. From some source, possibly the family reunions where the campaigns of the Civil War were refought endlessly, she also acquired a love for parades, waving flags, uniforms and martial music. During World War I, she did her part in Liberty Bond, Red Cross and Salvation Army drives and she served as a volunteer nurse for in-training soldiers during the flu epidemic. She had suitors galore, but her friends usually remarked that, if you wanted to marry Jean Faircloth, you had better put on a uniform.

As the years went by, Jean was engaged at least once, perhaps twice, but 1935 found her, heart and fancy free, boarding the S.S. *President Hoover* in San Francisco, bound for Shanghai on the first leg of a world cruise, a pretty, vivacious young woman who looked far younger than her thirty-six years.

On the voyage between Honolulu and Shanghai, Jean became the favorite of the MacArthur group, whose members found her an excellent dancer and "good fun." She dated and danced with the men impartially, including Eisenhower, but increasingly seemed to be spending more and more time with Douglas MacArthur. She never met his mother, on shipboard or in the Philippines, but did become good friends with Mary MacArthur, the widow of Admiral Arthur MacArthur, brother of Douglas, who was also aboard the *Hoover*.

And when the ship docked at Shanghai, brother and sister-in-law teamed up to persuade Jean to continue on the voyage to Manila for the inauguration of President Quezon and the attendant gay social season. Jean did continue on and her three-month stopover in Manila lengthened to six, then nine, and then twelve months. The Quezon inauguration provided the Islands with a reason for the gayest of festivals, and the pretty visitor from Murfreesboro was a familiar and popular part of them.

At first, she was seen with various beaux, but, as time went on, her partner came more and more to be General MacArthur. Until his mother died, two months after their arrival, he joined her at the parties and lavish balls. After his mother's death, they were seen less at the large affairs and even at the small, private parties they would usually slip away early—to go to the movies. MacArthur was an inveterate movie-goer, then and later, and evening after evening, frequently six nights a week, would find them in the back rows of the Manila film houses. If Jean Faircloth ever became bored with this routine—then or later—no one ever knew it.

Early in 1937, President Quezon asked MacArthur to accompany him on a governmental trip to Washington. The two sailed to Honolulu. Jean followed by plane a few days later and joined their ship there for the voyage to San Francisco. MacArthur went to Washington and Jean to Murfreesboro, where she shopped quietly for a trousseau.

Late in April, she left Murfreesboro (not to see her home again for thirteen years) and flew to Louisville. There she confided certain plans to a favorite aunt, who exclaimed that the people of America would certainly be surprised to learn that she was marrying General MacArthur.

"The people of Manila won't be," said Jean.

The couple met in New York and the next day, at 9:00 A.M., went to the Municipal Building, where they were married by a clerk, with Colonel T. J. Davis, a former aide, acting as best man. Both wore brown, and their wedding breakfast was bacon and eggs in the General's suite at the Waldorf. To reporters, MacArthur said, "This is going to last a long time."

In Manila, when the MacArthurs returned there late in May, the government had just completed a new five-story wing on the Manila Hotel, and the newlyweds moved into its more than roomy penthouse. There was a large formal drawing room, finished in gold décor, a library, a dining room and several bedrooms. There were balconies both in front and back. The one in the rear opened off the dining room and

overlooked the sea. It became a favorite spot of both Mac-
Arthurs, who formed the habit of spending the traditional
"Blue Hour" of the evening twilight there. They gave a formal
reception for several hundred on their return to Manila but
thereafter, except for small dinners, were content to spend
the evenings quietly, reading or watching films brought in
for private showings.

Their son, named Arthur in the MacArthur tradition, was
born February 21, 1938. His godparents were President and
Mrs. Quezon of the Philippines. Before his birth, Jean Mac-
Arthur had prayed for a son "to carry on the MacArthur military tradition." Long before he could read, little Arthur was
given a biography of Robert E. Lee.

Douglas MacArthur, quite naturally, was devoted to this
son and only child, born a month after his father's fifty-eighth
birthday. It was also quite natural, perhaps, that, according
to friends, the father should be more than ordinarily protective of the child, both then and in later years. The MacArthurs immediately obtained the services of the Chinese amah,
or nurse, Ah Cheu, who quickly became an integral part of
the family and who made the escape dash with them from
Corregidor to Australia. At this writing, she still makes her
home with Mrs. MacArthur and Arthur, who, contrary to the
MacArthur tradition, has never evinced any interest in a military career.

By midsummer of 1941, the portents of a major war in the
Pacific were becoming unmistakable. Japan had invaded
Indo-China in the autumn of 1940, and the Philippines stood
directly in the path of the Nipponese avowed drive to extend
her Asian empire. On July 26, 1941, President Roosevelt
recalled MacArthur to active duty in the rank of major general and placed him in command of the United States Armed
Forces of the Far East. The following day, he was promoted

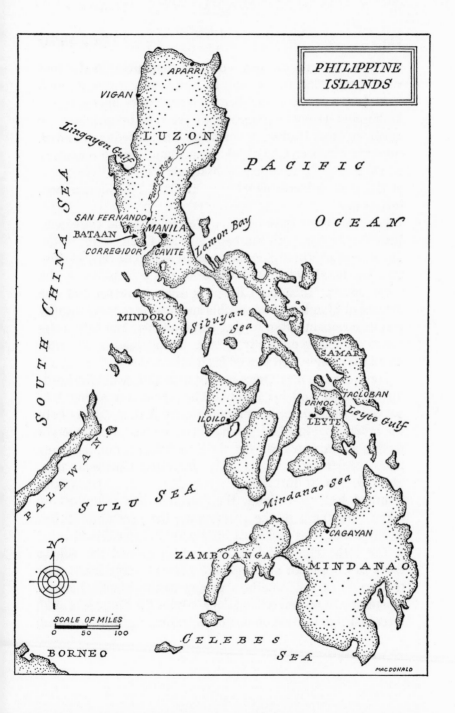

to lieutenant general and, not long thereafter, to the four
stars of full general, the rank he had held as Chief of Staff.

At 4:00 A.M. on December 7 (it was December 8 in the
Philippines), General MacArthur learned by telephone of the
attack on Pearl Harbor. A few hours later, shortly after noon,
came the attack on Clark Field, near Manila, and the destruction of half of the American military air fleet. The destruction
of the United States naval base at Cavite, in Manila Bay,
followed.

For the sixteen days between December 8 and Christmas,
Jean MacArthur, with the baby and Ah Cheu, watched the
Japanese planes dropping their bombs in Manila Bay, so close
that her hotel building shook from the concussion of the
bomb blasts. Then on Christmas Eve, knowing that the
defense of Manila was impossible and hoping to spare the city
and its occupants from further aerial attacks, MacArthur declared Manila an open city, that is, an undefended city, with
no military value, and moved his headquarters to Corregidor.

President and Mrs. Quezon went with him, as did the headquarters staff and his family. When Jean MacArthur had
packed a suitcase for herself and one for Arthur, adding only
the brown coat in which she had been married, the General's
medals and Arthur's tricycle, she closed the door on the penthouse apartment with its gaily decorated Christmas tree,
never to see its furnishings again. When the MacArthurs
returned four years later, the Japanese had destroyed or
taken everything in the place, with the exception of the
family silver. This had been hidden by Filipino friends.

The little inter-island steamer which carried the official
party to Corregidor also took along several large boxes containing all of the American money in the Manila banks—
amounting to several million dollars—plus the Philippine gold
reserve. From his seat on one of the boxes, a guard remarked

that he would gladly trade it all, at that moment, for a few square feet of American soil.

Corregidor at that time was roughly divided into three areas: Topside, where the officers were quartered and where the heavy artillery guarded Manila Bay; Bottomside, where Malinta Tunnel, wide enough for two automobiles to drive abreast, had been bored through solid rock; and Middleside, the portion of the island just above the tunnel.

The MacArthurs spent their first night on Corregidor in the tunnel, which had offshoots containing a hospital, offices and sleeping quarters. The second night they and the Quezons moved into the local commander's quarters Topside. It took the Japanese just four days to discover that the General had moved to Corregidor and where his quarters were located there. On December 29, about 8:00 A.M., a flight of eighteen enemy bombers made one pass over Topside and then staged a four-hour bombing performance.

When the sirens sounded, Jean MacArthur grabbed Arthur and, with Ah Cheu, took refuge in a small and inadequate dugout down the hill from the commander's house. Holding the boy in her arms, she huddled against the back wall, watching the dugout doors, which would not close, swing and bang with every bomb blast.

Other members of the group still tell the story of MacArthur's reaction to the raid, which he took as a personal affront. Refusing to take shelter, he first stood on the front lawn of the commander's quarters, hands on hips, counting the bombers. Then, moving to the dubious shelter of a hedge, he watched every bomb fall. One direct hit went through his bedroom, demolishing the whole house and sending fragments of steel and debris flying across the lawn.

His orderly, Sergeant Domingo Adversario, crouched close to the General, taking off his own helmet so that it would, he said later, "cover both of us a little." One bit of steel struck the helmet. Another wounded Adversario in the hand. The raid ended with no casualties, but Topside was a mass of torn, smoking rubble and everyone moved Bottomside.

The days went on, with Topside both untenable and demolished. The MacArthurs moved into a small house about a mile from the Malinta Tunnel. Quarters were also arranged for them in the tunnel itself, and Jean MacArthur took young Arthur and Ah Cheu there during the frequent air raids. A car with a Filipino driver was always available. During the day, the driver was located in the vehicle. At night, he slept in a foxhole a few feet away. When the sirens sounded, Mrs. MacArthur bustled her little family into the automobile and rushed to the tunnel. Sometimes it would happen two or three times a night. General MacArthur never went with her.

On January 20, there was a birthday party for MacArthur, his sixty-second, and on February 21 another for Arthur, complete with a cake and four candles. On January 30, there was an inauguration ceremony for President Quezon, and he was sworn in for a second term as President of the Commonwealth of the Philippines. Although quite ill with tuberculosis, Quezon made an inaugural address and then MacArthur concluded the "program" with a moving talk on the trials which lay ahead for the Philippine nation, and of the road back to victory and peace. Not long thereafter, Quezon and his family, along with other members of the Corregidor party, were taken off the island by submarine, headed for Australia. Washington advised at this time that perhaps MacArthur would like to evacuate his wife and son.

Jean MacArthur answered no. "We three are as one," she said, in a much-quoted sentence. "We drink from the same cup."

Throughout all of this time, of course, General MacArthur

had been directing the defense of Bataan, utilizing his intimate familiarity with the tortuous terrain of the peninsula to hold and block the superior Japanese forces. And throughout all these dark, depressing days, he had never given up hope that his holding action there was only until ground, air and navy reinforcements could arrive from America. Temporary losses and setbacks he could understand, but defeat was both a term and a condition virtually unthinkable. It was not until late in February, when messages arrived ordering him to escape by the most expeditious manner to Australia, that he accepted the reality of American war policy in 1942. The men and ships and supplies which might have driven the Japanese from the Philippines were being sent to Europe instead.

MacArthur was deeply upset over the orders directing him to leave embattled Bataan and Corregidor, and, for a time, he considered refusing to obey them. In the end, however, he gave in and on March 11, 1942, with his family, Ah Cheu * and fourteen members of his staff set off in the PT boats for the escape to Australia which is recounted in an earlier chapter.

* Much has been made of MacArthur's taking the Chinese amah, instead of perhaps an American nurse. For one thing, as the late Colonel Sid Huff, MacArthur's aide, has pointed out, none of the nurses would have gone. They were military, they were greatly needed on Corregidor and it was a matter of duty. Ah Cheu, a Chinese civilian, was in no way covered by the protective war clauses of the Geneva Convention; rather, as a close member of the MacArthur family, she would probably have been subjected to special tortures by the Japanese, a fact MacArthur well knew.

11

Macarthur had left one bleak situation in the Philippines. His American and Philippine forces on Bataan and Corregidor were near annihilation by the overwhelming strength of the Japanese forces.

He found another when he arrived in Australia. The enemy had taken Hong Kong, Singapore, Java, Borneo, Indo-China and New Britain, just above New Guinea. With the surrender of the Philippines, which was inevitable unless help reached them in a matter of days or weeks, the Japanese would have full control of the Pacific from Japan south to New Guinea—and New Guinea was the wide front door to Australia. Already the Nipponese bombers were raiding Port Moresby, on the north coast of New Guinea and Darwin on the south coast of Australia. New Guinea was clearly marked as the next target—with Australia to follow.

MacArthur had arrived expecting to find troops, war planes and ships massed in strength for a quick and powerful drive to relieve the Philippines. Instead, he found forces so inadequate that the Australian military leaders despaired of even defending that continent from the expected invasion. They had drawn a line across Australia at Brisbane. This they planned to defend in a last-ditch stand. New Guinea was to be virtually undefended. All of Australia north of the Brisbane line would be abandoned, with a total destruction of everything there which might give aid and comfort to the enemy.

MacArthur was appalled when he discovered the forces available to him—some twenty-five thousand American Army troops, a weary and understrength Australian division (the cream of the Australian Army was fighting in Europe), a handful of combat aircraft, most of them out of commission, and no Navy to speak of.

If he found this "the greatest surprise and shock of the war," he was equally dismayed at the Australian plan to retreat back of the Brisbane line.

"Such a concept," he told the Australian chiefs of staff, "is fatal to every possibility of ever assuming the offensive. Even if tactically successful, it would bottle us up on the Australian continent, probably permanently." He was determined to abandon the plan completely.

On April 14, a month after his arrival, he had been made Supreme Commander of the Southwest Pacific Theater and a few weeks later he received the news that Bataan and Corregidor had fallen. It brought him, as he said, a sadness from which he never recovered. It also strengthened his resolve to let nothing stop his drive back across the Pacific to recapture the Philippines.

In Prime Minister John Curtain, a rough-and-ready former union labor leader, MacArthur found a firm ally. The two men hit it off well together and became fast friends. The MacArthur name, the MacArthur reputation and the MacArthur attitude also inspired the Australian people and won over the military leaders.

The situation was desperate, the General admitted. In any action the Allies would be outnumbered five to one. They were pitiably short of men and the machines of war—but to retreat was unthinkable.

They would attack. It was a decision characteristic of Mac-Arthur.

His plan was as bold as the circumstances were desperate. It was to move the Allied defense line fifteen hundred miles north and forward into New Guinea and there to stop the Japanese on the Owen Stanley Mountains which range up to thirteen thousand feet the length of the island.

His first step was to move his headquarters from Melbourne to Brisbane, some eight hundred miles nearer the scene of action. He made shifts in command and notably brought in a new air commander—short, tough, bristle-haired Major General George Kenney.

He divided his campaign into phases. The first, designed to prevent the invasion of Australia, was to stop the Japanese in the Owen Stanley Mountains. The second was to drive "arrow-straight" from New Guinea (once it was taken) to the Philippines.

MacArthur moved his headquarters from Melbourne to Brisbane on July 20, 1942, and, at the same time, established an advance headquarters at Port Moresby on the south coast of New Guinea. The Japanese selected the next day to land a large amphibious force at Buna and Gona, just across the island. They immediately started a drive across the Owen Stanley Mountains.

Their route was over the Kokoda trail, which would lead them directly into Port Moresby. Had Port Moresby fallen, Australia would have been next.

The Australian troops defending the mountain trails, outnumbered four and five to one by the Japanese, gave way, fighting desperately for every inch of terrain. The Japanese were veteran, hand-picked troops. They wore green uniforms which blended with the foliage, painted their hands and faces green and used every trick of deception and infiltration.

From his advance headquarters at Port Moresby, a low rambling house which had been the home of the governor before the war, MacArthur saw the fighting at first hand—fighting over terrain which has been described as like no other in the world.

New Guinea is a tenth the size of the United States, and its altitude and climate varies from steaming jungle to freezing mountaintops. Its mountain trails are so rugged that troops often could travel no more than half a mile a day. Each path is "booby-trapped" by twisted roots and bordered by waist-deep odorous slime. During rains—and the New Guinea jungle has an average of one hundred and seventy inches of rainfall annually, compared with twenty-nine inches annually in the United States—the trails become streaming, racing rivers.

In the air were clouds of mosquitoes which the men breathed and ate and fought off. The ground and the leaves and branches of the trees and underbrush swarmed with biting ants, fleas, poisonous spiders, a hundred unidentified insects and bugs—and vividly hued butterflies that drank the sweat from men's bodies. Their colors were only rivaled by the birds which screamed and scolded from jungle tree perches, contrasting with the blackness of darting, evil-looking bats. In the swamps were crocodiles and snakes—the latter ranging from tiny poisonous varieties to the twenty-five-foot constrictors.

Men scratched the insect bites until they turned into festering sores and sweated off twenty and more pounds until they came down with any of a dozen tropical diseases—blackwater or dengue fever, dysentery, typhus, ringworm, hookworm or the yaws, a contagious and terrible skin disease known medically as frambesia.

As the Australians gave ground slowly, MacArthur knew that he had not the men to fight on even terms; he must instead outsmart and outmaneuver the enemy. In September, he sensed that the Japanese commander would try to outflank Port Moresby with a landing at Milne Bay on the southeast tip of New Guinea. He moved his forces in secretly, two Australian brigades and thirteen hundred American soldiers. The unsuspecting Japanese tried to land at what they thought was an undefended coastal point, ran into deadly fire and were decisively defeated. The battle lasted a week and, when the enemy retired, he left seven hundred dead and all of his equipment ashore. It was the first Allied ground victory in the Pacific and gave a badly needed lift to the war effort.

With this success behind him, MacArthur then planned a master stroke—striking the Japanese along their flank and rear on the northern New Guinea coast. It was an incredibly ambitious undertaking. MacArthur had no amphibious craft, almost no seacraft of any kind. His reserve troops, then in training, were in Brisbane, almost fifteen hundred miles from the fighting front. Repeated pleas to Washington brought no promises of naval craft before November, and MacArthur had timed his operation for October, when the Japanese would have stretched their supply points to the breaking point.

He may have remembered the famous "taxicab army" of World War I, when the French used thousands of Paris taxis to rush reinforcements to stop the Germans at the Battle of the Marne, or his own desperate "sideslip" into Bataan. In any event, he commandeered every available craft in Australia, down to ferryboats and river steamers. He converted the few warships under his command into troop carriers. Every vessel was loaded to its capacity with fighting men bound from Brisbane to New Guinea.

This solved half the battle plan, but did not solve the problem of getting an attacking force to the north coast of New Guinea. At this point MacArthur made an historical decision. Could an attacking force be airlifted over the mountains and landed on grass strips near Buna and Gona, which the Japanese held? He turned to his air commander, General Kenney.

"Give me a few days to prepare," said Kenney, "and I'll move a whole division if you want it." As it turned out, he moved two divisions.

The rest of the staff doubted that it could be done. They voiced their negative views strongly. Then Kenney presented his plan in the usual forceful Kenney manner. MacArthur listened to both sides. Finally, he thanked the other staff members politely for their advice—and told Kenney to go ahead.

Kenney took a leaf from the boss's book. He commandeered every airplane he could get his hands on, including civilian airliners. Using transport planes and his weary old B-17s, Kenney flew in thousands of men, more than a million tons of food, weapons and ammunition—including 105-mm howitzers and horses to pull them. When the weather closed in over the Owen Stanley Mountains, the pilots remarked that the "clouds are full of rocks today," but they kept on flying and many a GI was surprised to be greeted by General MacArthur when he arrived on the landing strip.

Kenney worked out a system for dropping supplies by parachute, and when the weather went bad for several days on end, countered with a system of blind delivery. Elated, he

went to MacArthur's headquarters at Port Moresby to tell
him about it. Kenney relates the story in his book, *The Mac-
Arthur I Know:*

"George," said MacArthur, "you know there are a lot of
men over there eating their last meal tonight."

"Yes," Kenney replied, "but tomorrow we serve breakfast
at six-thirty and by noon I'll have five days' rations over to
them."

He then explained that the pilots had worked out a system
for the three-hundred-pound food drops in foggy weather.
Operating on instruments, the pilot flew toward the airstrip
radio station, using his radio compass for directions. When
the plane passed directly over the radio station, the needle of
the compass flipped. At that moment, the pilot signaled the
man in the rear of the plane. He shoved the bundle of food
out the door. The plane then circled and repeated the process
until the entire load was delivered.

A check run, Kenney told MacArthur, had put sixteen
bundles, dropped from twenty-five hundred feet up, within
a circle one hundred yards in diameter.

In spite of a thousand almost insurmountable difficulties,
the world's worst terrain and devilish weather, MacArthur
put two divisions exactly where he wanted them and supplied them almost entirely by air. It was a feat, the first of its
kind in military history, which was copied later in the
European Theater. With today's techniques it would be
commonplace. Then, it was heroic, dangerous and daring.
Said Kenney:

It was a large order for our pitifully small Air Force, but I
believed we could do it. MacArthur believed we could do it and
gave the go-ahead in spite of the adverse recommendations of his
whole staff. The campaign was not an easy one. Many times, in

spite of everything the Air Force could do, victory hung in the balance, but MacArthur stood by his decision and backed me and the Air Force when his staff would willingly have abandoned the advance on Buna and recommended me for incarceration in an insane asylum.

A lesser man could have lost his head and become panicky on many occasions, but throughout the campaign, MacArthur's coolness and decisiveness were an inspiration to his staff and his commanders.

The airlift was not the only innovation MacArthur and his men evolved to "equalize" the disparity in numbers between Japanese and Allied troops. Fragmentation bombs were rigged to parachutes and exploded overhead, killing literally hundreds of enemy troops in one attack. Light bombers were rigged with so many machine guns for strafing that the recoil popped rivets from the skin of the fuselage.

With the divisions landed north of Buna pressing in and with the Australian troops in the mountains pressing down, MacArthur now began the squeeze play which routed the enemy and forever ended the threat to Port Moresby and Australia.

By heavily reinforcing the Australians, he drove the Japanese off the mountain trails and back to the north coast. There they dug into well-prepared positions around Buna and Gona, sunken fortresses lined with sand-filled oil drums and so well camouflaged with vines and palm leaves as to be virtually undetectable. Hidden at every strategic point were the deadly snipers. It was desperate jungle warfare against an enemy who fought fanatically and never surrendered. The campaign bogged down and MacArthur watched for weeks while his drive stalled in a stalemate of attrition.

Then he sent for Lieutenant General Eichelberger, who had been training the troops sent against the Japanese. It was

November 30, 1942. MacArthur told him, "I'm putting you in command at Buna. I want you to remove all officers who won't fight. Relieve regimental and battalion commanders if you see fit. If necessary, put sergeants in charge of battalions and corporals in charge of companies. Put in any man who will fight. Take Buna."

Eichelberger stopped attacking for two days while he reorganized the whole command structure. He devised new tactics, improved the food and medical supply lines. He let his three stars be seen in the front lines and manned a machine gun against enemy snipers. A sergeant who led a squad of men through to the Buna beach was made a captain on the spot and given the Distinguished Service Cross. The morale changed and so did the offensive action. On December 14, two weeks after changing commanders, MacArthur could announce that Buna village had fallen.

There was still much fighting to clear the area, but the back of the Japanese resistance was broken. In one desperate effort to retrieve the situation, the enemy made an attack in strength against a small airfield at Wau, held by a small contingent of Australians.

Greatly outnumbered, the defenders fell back from their advance posts toward the airstrip, an important advance field in MacArthur's future plans. Knowing he could not get troops there in time overland, MacArthur dispatched reinforcements by air, and the action took on the aspects of an old-time movie thriller.

The Allied troops were defending one end of the landing strip and the Japanese were attacking at the other when the troop ships landed. The Australian reinforcements leaped from their planes, firing as they came. With fifty-seven plane loads—the entire 17th Australian Brigade—they drove the enemy back into the jungles within twenty-four hours.

Another Japanese attempt to halt MacArthur's drive came in the form of massive reinforcements for the Buna area. Using transports and destroyer escorts, the Japanese steamed out of Raboul on February 28. By March 1, the convoy was spotted and what followed became the Battle of the Bismarck Sea. It lasted three days and was completely a struggle between Japanese sea power and MacArthur's land-based aircraft. No allied naval craft were involved. Here again came one of the innovations of the war—skip bombing.

Kenney's pilots had been practicing the maneuver against the half-sunken hulks in Port Moresby harbor and had perfected its techniques. Skip bombing consisted of attacking a ship at low level, aiming at the craft's broad hull and "skipping" the bomb against it—the same game that every small boy has played, skipping rocks across a pond. The art of skip bombing combined the advantages of torpedo and dive bombing while effecting a broader target to the pilot.

MacArthur's victory claims, made on the reports of General Kenney's Fifth Air Force, were disputed at the time, but captured reports later showed them to be realistic. There were from seven to thirteen thousand Japanese soldiers in the convoy. Only eight hundred and fifty got through to land on New Guinea. Eight transports and four destroyers were sunk, more than half the Japanese soldiers were killed and immense supplies of food, ammunition and fuel were lost.

The Buna victory did not end the battle for the north New Guinea coast, but it was a signal victory for MacArthur and his forces. Early that January of 1943, Secretary of War Stimson cabled him:

The coming of the New Year, coinciding as it does with your success at Buna, impels me again to send you my warmest congratulations and good wishes. Have followed your masterly campaign with close interest and much gratification. It is a tremendous satisfaction to feel that American fortunes in the Southwest Pacific are in such skillful hands; am in constant touch with President Quezon here and we are both beginning to think with encouragement of the time, which now really seems approaching, when we shall redeem our promise to the Filipinos.

The Japanese still held the major portion of New Guinea and also, of course, the neighboring island of New Britain. The latter was important for two major reasons—its big port and supply point, Rabaul, and the fact that it helped command the vital Vitiez Strait. The Japanese still held Lae, Finschafen and Salamaua, on the New Guinea side of the Strait. Between these strong points and the fortifications at Cape Gloucester on the New Britain side, the Japanese were able to block the passage of Allied convoys from Australia northward.

The New Year brought other bright spots on the war horizon. Based on his experiences during his first few months in Australia, MacArthur had advocated a single commander in the Pacific, offering to take a subordinate position in such a command. This eventuality did not take place until much later in the war, but on February 8, 1943, Guadalcanal fell to the American Marines and in March of 1943, the Third American Fleet, under Admiral William "Bull" Halsey, was placed under MacArthur's control.

Then, in April, one of the most significant events of the war occurred. The American intelligence staff had broken the most secret Japanese code. Intercepted messages in mid-April revealed that Admiral Isoroku Yamamoto, Commander-in-Chief of the Japanese Combined Fleet, had scheduled a flight from Rabaul to the Solomons.

The Admiral took off at 6:00 A.M., on April 18, flying a Japanese "Betty" bomber with nine escort fighters. At 7:30

they were hit by sixteen American "Lightning" fighters. Captain Thomas G. Lamphier, flying one of the Lightnings, shot down the Admiral's plane. It crashed in flames, killing Yamamoto and three members of his staff.

The first targets of MacArthur's 1943 offensive were two small islands, Woodlark and Kiriwina, off the southeastern tip of New Guinea. These fell quickly. The capture of Lae followed, along with Salamaua and Finschafen a little later.

The assault on Lae, September 5, saw the first use of a major paratrooper force in the Pacific. The plan of assault was a characteristic MacArthur tactic of striking the target on the flanks and avoiding a direct and costly frontal attack.

While an amphibious force landed to the east of Lae, the paratroopers were dropped into the Markham Valley, west of the town. Some three hundred planes took part in the action. A contingent of B-25 two-engine bombers armed with fifty-caliber machine guns led the way in to the cleared landing strips. They were followed by A-20 attack planes, which laid down a smoke screen for the paratroopers.

Next in line came the *Bataan*, MacArthur's B-17, carrying MacArthur himself. Following it in was another B-17 with General Kenney. Then some one hundred transport planes flew in, dropping the paratroopers and a full battery of artillery. MacArthur went along because, as he said, "I did not want our paratroops to enter their first combat fraught with such hazard without such comfort as my presence might bring to them."

After the drop had been completed and their temporary position secured, MacArthur radioed his wife in Brisbane, "It was a honey."

Records from his headquarters files tell the story of the operation:

Transport after transport poured out its cargo of fully equipped paratroopers upon the vital airstrip. Watching the multi-colored parachutes spread themselves over the valley, General MacArthur felt the satisfaction of seeing this daring operation carried out with smooth precision. Even before he left the scene the ground was being prepared for the big transports [to land] as flame throwers began to eat away the large patches of tall kunai grass. On the next day, the first of the planes bearing elements of the 7th Division landed on the runway to discharge its precious load of troops and equipment.

The Japanese were surrounded except for one narrow route of escape northward through the dense jungles and almost impassable mountain trails of the Huon Peninsula. As the Allied noose gradually choked them off from all hope of aid, the Japanese yielded their positions and, discarding almost all equipment, began a precipitous flight through jungle and mountains toward Kiari in a desperate effort to escape complete annihilation. On 16 September, Lae was occupied by the Allies.

The year ended with MacArthur pressing westward, back along the trail to the Philippines. By February 10, 1944, the last Japanese forces were driven out of eastern New Guinea. With swift attacks, Allied troops had taken the Green Islands, north of Bougainville, and the Admiralties in the Bismarck Archipelago. The big port of Rabaul was encircled, bypassed, left useless.

"I don't want it," said MacArthur. "Let it starve."

In April of 1944, the General leap-frogged five hundred miles ahead, capturing Hollandia and Aitape, in surprise assaults, striking both positions with landing forces of sixty-two thousand men and entrapping thousands of Japanese soldiers who fled inland and then died in suicidal counter-attacks.

So sure were the Japanese that MacArthur would strike elsewhere that Admiral Yoshikazu Endo, Commander of the

Japanese Eighth and Ninth Fleets, had gone to Hollandia by submarine for safety. He watched the landings on the beach below him from an armchair in his quarters, then put on his dress uniform, walked into the jungle and killed himself.

Jumping another two hundred miles west, MacArthur took Wakde and then Biak Island, still further along the line. The last enemy stronghold on New Guinea was the Vogelkop Peninsula. With a landing and victory there late in August, 1944, the last resistance on New Guinea had ended. Douglas MacArthur was now within six hundred miles of the Philippines.

12

GENERAL Douglas MacArthur designed his own cap when he was made Chief of Staff in 1930. It followed the usual pattern of an officer's cap, but its front peak was a little higher, its gold embroidery a little heavier, its army eagle a little angrier, its cant a little jauntier.

That cap became the most famous in the world. MacArthur had long ago set the pattern of never wearing a helmet. During World War I, he removed the wire grommet from his regulation hat, wrapped a nonregulation woolen muffler (for a chronic sore throat) around his neck and took both into the trenches and on patrols under fire.

As that World War I figure became familiar to the doughboys of the Rainbow Division, so MacArthur in his tan, battered but always jaunty cap became relatively commonplace to the men of three services fighting the MacArthur war in the Pacific.

It was soaked by the sea spray churned up by the PT boats on his escape from Corregidor and shrank until it would barely perch on the top of his head. In Melbourne, an aide scoured the city to find a cap stretcher and brought the cap back to proper size.

Years later, in Japan, when it was practically falling to pieces, Tokyo's most skilled cap-maker tried in vain to duplicate it, but the color, the slant, the insouciance of his copies were never quite right. Finally, a worn khaki shirt, faded to just the proper shade, was pressed into service to cover the original chassis. The General was content. He wore it the rest of his life.

To the cap and the carelessly open collar was added the MacArthur corncob pipe (adopted after he gave up cigarettes for his throat's sake) to complete a figure that was distinguishable anywhere. The pipe has an extra long stem and bowl.

During World War I, as a brigadier, he earned a dozen decorations for personal bravery in combat where personal bravery meant virtually hand-to-hand combat. When his staff remonstrated, he had replied that nothing better for the morale of the American troops could happen than having a general officer killed in combat.

During the war in the Pacific, MacArthur was equally casual of his personal safety and the fact that his cap, his corncob pipe and his four stars made him a perfect target for enemy snipers, who always preferred to get the officers when they could.

From Corregidor, the General would surprise the men fighting in the Bataan jungles by showing up at an outpost rifle pit, plus cap and corncob pipe, smiling and apparently oblivious of any danger. When a flight of Jap bombers came over and the troops scurried for cover, they looked up from slit trenches to find MacArthur standing in the open, feet apart, studying the bombing formation through glasses.

From Port Moresby, he climbed the trails up the Owen Stanley Range with the Australian troops in the kind of personal reconnaissance he could and would not forgo. General

Kenney relates that one of the first stories he heard when he arrived in Australia in the summer of 1942 was that MacArthur was afraid to fly:

It had never dawned on me that he was afraid of anything but I thought it would be a good idea to debunk the story. [The target of many detractors, MacArthur had not been popular with Kenney's young flyers. They had been told he did not appreciate air power and also that he had voted to convict Billy Mitchell, neither of which report was true. As a good subordinate, Kenney set out to "sell" MacArthur to "his kids" in the Pacific theater. Since MacArthur had a very high appreciation of air power indeed and showed it by both utilization and high praise, Kenney succeeded.]

Kenney continued:

So, one evening in September, I casually remarked to the General in Brisbane that I was going to New Guinea again soon to inspect the air units there and would like to have him come along also to look over the show. He replied instantly, "All right. Let's leave tomorrow. I'll be your guest."

We took off early the next morning in my B-17 bomber. The ceiling was only about five hundred feet, but the cloud layer was not very thick and soon we were on top at six thousand feet and on our way to New Guinea. The General watched the play of the sunlight on the clouds for a while and then settled back in his chair for a nap.

I left him and went up to the front cockpit of the plane. About a hundred miles out of Brisbane the oil pressure on one of the engines suddenly dropped to zero. I told the pilot to shut off that engine, feather the propeller and return to Brisbane to see what was the matter. The B-17 would fly on three engines if the fourth quit, but I didn't see any sense in starting out on a sixteen-hundred-mile over-water flight with something wrong. I went back to where MacArthur was still sleeping peacefully. I touched his knee. He opened his eyes, smiled and said:

"I guess I must have dozed off. Do you want something?"

"Oh, nothing in particular," Kenney replied, "I just wanted to tell you that this is a good airplane." MacArthur nodded. "In fact," Kenney went on, "it flies almost as well on three engines as it does on four."

"I like to listen to you enthusiastic aviators," said MacArthur, "even when you exaggerate a little."

"All right," said Kenney, "we've been flying on three engines for the last twenty minutes and you didn't know it. In fact, you didn't even wake up. If you look out that window, you can see the propeller of number two engine standing still."

MacArthur looked out the window, listened carefully for a while, grinned and said, "Nice comfortable feeling, isn't it?" and leaned back in his seat and relaxed.

"He took it a lot more coolly than I did the first time I had a bomber engine quit," relates Kenney. The plane continued back to Brisbane, where the engine was repaired, and the next day Kenney and MacArthur flew back to Port Moresby. Most of the flight was through heavy rain. It took six hours.

"MacArthur slept through three of them," said Kenney.

A year later, MacArthur accompanied the paradrop operation to capture Lae on the north coast of New Guinea, as related earlier. He was flying with then Colonel Roger Ramey, in another B-17. Fifteen minutes out of Port Moresby an engine quit and Ramey sent his copilot back to MacArthur to inform him of that fact.

"That's all right," MacArthur replied. "Tell Colonel Ramey to carry on. I've been with General Kenney when one engine quit and I know the B-17 flies almost as well on three engines as on four. Tell him not to worry about me. I know he wants to see the show too."

So, the familiar tan hat and corncob pipe were waiting for the first paratroopers when they landed to make the assault on Lae, twenty-five miles away.

The stories told of MacArthur's coolness and complete disregard of danger are almost endless. In February, 1944, his forces seized the Admiralty Islands with an initial landing force of a thousand men. MacArthur went along. Because General Kenney had evinced great interest in the landing field there, General MacArthur examined it closely. He stepped it off in length and width and then dug into the surface to see how good the construction was—all while an anguished aide was trying to get both the general and himself out of the range of sniper fire which was growing heavier as the Japanese resistance dug in.

At the Brunei Bay operation in the capture of British Borneo, in June of 1945, after the Philippines had been retaken, MacArthur went ashore with the second wave and led a group of staff members along a road paralleling the beach.

"An occasional sniper's shot and a burst of machine gun fire ahead of us and farther inland kept the trip from being too boring," Kenney, a member of the party, declares.

The party stopped while MacArthur chatted with a patrol and stepped aside to let a tank pass. Fifty yards ahead, the tank halted to clear out an enemy machine gun nest. MacArthur walked on. There were two dead Japanese soldiers in the road. MacArthur inspected their clothing and equipment, remarking on the excellence of it. A photographer came up and wanted to take his picture with the two bodies. MacArthur declined. The cameraman then photographed the two dead soldiers and got a bullet in his shoulder as the flashbulb popped. The staff finally talked MacArthur into turning back, persuading him that, as a guest on shipboard, he shouldn't be late for dinner.

General Kenney tells another and lighter story of his association with General MacArthur. As a long-time San Franciscan, Kenney was friendly with Dan London, manager of the St. Francis Hotel, and had dinner with him the night before leaving to join MacArthur in 1942.

London was lamenting that he had just lost his chef to the military draft. "He's the best cook in the country," said London, "and the darned fools in the army don't even know it. They've got him mowing lawns or something in Honolulu."

Kenney, who puts good food in second place behind good airplanes, made careful inquiries as to the man's name—George Raymond—and his military outfit. He discovered that Raymond was serving under an old friend.

"I wanted to get Raymond," said Kenney, "but I knew I had to be very careful. This general he worked for is a mean trader."

When Kenney landed in Honolulu, the friend met him at the airport and invited Kenney to stay at his quarters. After some usual Air Force conversation and note-trading, Kenney began an elaborate story. It concerned some old friends in New England. They had been neighbors and he had seen them on a recent trip. They had mentioned a son—a boy named George Raymond, who had, actually, been named after George Kenney. They had asked Kenney if he wouldn't look after him. Kenney had thought, he said casually, that he might just take the boy, his namesake, under his wing.

"So you want one of my men," said his friend suspiciously. "What's so good about him that you want to steal him?" Kenney protested that it was purely a friendship matter, just that, and, after all, as he understood it, the soldier wasn't doing anything much there.

In the end, Kenney traded his friend an aircraft mechanic (he had first wanted a crew chief) for Raymond and took him along to Australia. There Kenney set him up in his quarters in charge of pantry and kitchen.

"The man was marvelous," said Kenney. "He could turn

army rations into a meal that even Dan London would have been glad to eat. And it didn't take long for MacArthur to make this discovery. He had a pretty good cook at home—Jean MacArthur—but he found it very convenient many a day to drop into my quarters about mealtime."

13

☆ ☆ ☆ ☆ ☆

THE COSTLY and bitter frontal campaign against Buna, where the troops were dug into highly fortified jungle positions, had been necessary. Buna had to be taken before the rest of New Guinea could be cleared, but the losses in terms of time and men influenced greatly MacArthur's conduct of his war in the Pacific thereafter.

From the lessons of Buna he designed and refined what was to become his famous "hit-'em-where-they-ain't" strategy and style of warfare. The most notable example was Rabaul, on New Britain. This great port was the nerve and supply center of Japanese operations in the South Pacific. It held hundreds of aircraft on five airfields, approximately one hundred thousand Japanese troops and mountains of supplies. Its harbor was a busy traffic center for convoys and shipping.

To attack it would have required an immense force, with resulting staggering losses in men and supplies. Equally important, such a campaign could have taken months, as Guadacanal had. Instead, MacArthur took the more lightly held points surrounding Rabaul, isolated it, cut it off from supplies, had Kenney bomb it in heavy strikes—and left it, in his own words, "to die on the vine." He said:

"My strategic conception for the Pacific Theater," he said, "contemplates massive strokes against only main strategic objectives, utilizing surprise and air-ground striking power, supported and assisted by the fleet. This is the very opposite of what is termed 'island hopping,' which is the gradual pushing back of the enemy by direct frontal pressure with the consequential heavy casualties which will certainly be involved.

"Key points must of course be taken, but a wise choice of such will obviate the need for storming the mass of islands now in enemy possession. 'Island hopping' with extravagant losses and slow progress is not my idea of how to win a war as soon and as cheaply as possible. New conditions require for solution, and new weapons require for maximum application, new and imaginative weapons. Wars are never won in the past."

MacArthur never took credit for developing his particular strategy.

"It is as old as war itself," he said. "It is merely a new name, dictated by new conditions, given to the ancient principle of envelopment.

"This just happens to be the first time that the area of combat has embraced land and water in such relative proportions. In this war, we are applying the concept of envelopment to a new type of battleground. It has always proved the ideal method for success by inferior in number but faster moving forces."

MacArthur always felt that the success of his aerial envelopment of Buna by paradrop, and its later capture, marked the turning part of the war.

"From this point on," he said, "it was no longer a question of whether the Japanese would be beaten; now the only question was how and how long."

He demonstrated his "hit-em-where-they-ain't" technique in a dozen different swift moves after Buna. Sure that Mac-

Arthur would strike for Rabaul, the Japanese prepared elaborate defenses there, while he struck at Arawe, on the distant southeastern end of New Britain, and then at Cape Gloucester on the western tip. Then he took the two neighboring islands, Green and Emirau, and Rabaul was surrounded.

When he took Hollandia, the enemy was braced for him at the big naval base of Wewak. He had made elaborate plans to attack Wewak—and had purposely allowed the plan to leak to the enemy. Then he bypassed the naval base and hit Hollandia, farther down the coast. From Hollandia he could cut all Japanese supply routes to New Guinea, including Wewak.

When MacArthur had cleared New Guinea, his next logical step was the island of Halmahera, just off the northeastern tip of New Guinea and directly on the path to the Philippines. It was such a logical next step that the Japanese fortified it strongly and concentrated thousands of troops there.

Bypassing it completely, the MacArthur forces landed instead at Moratai, nearly a hundred miles nearer the Philippines, against almost no resistance. Again, cut off from supplies, the Japanese on Halmahera were left to starve uselessly, resorting to cannibalism before they finally surrendered.

And now MacArthur was within three hundred miles of his goal, the Philippine Islands. In twenty-two months, according to one historian, he had taken more territory with smaller loss of life than any commander since Darius the Great, who reigned in Persia 2,500 years ago.

In July of 1944, MacArthur was ordered to go to Pearl Harbor for a conference. His message from General Marshall, head of the combined chiefs of staff in Washington, gave no details of who else would be present, nor of the subject to be discussed. Why this omission was made has never been explained.

When General MacArthur reached Honolulu, he learned that President Roosevelt was there and that the purpose of the conference was to determine the next course of action against Japan. Although previous Pacific war plans had all embodied MacArthur's drive to the Philippines, he now found another course of action proposed.

With Franklin Roosevelt a quiet listener, Admiral Chester Nimitz, Central Pacific commander, presented the Navy's proposal. In general it was to bypass the Philippines and attack Formosa. All of MacArthur's forces, with token exceptions, were to be transferred to Nimitz. The Admiral's plan was well organized with charts, maps and supporting papers. He would be ready to invade Formosa by the summer of 1945, he said.

MacArthur had taken one aide to the conference with him. He had brought no maps, no charts, no prepared presentation.

When the Navy's presentation was finished, MacArthur picked up a pointer and walked over to the map. There, without raising his voice, without gestures or dramatics of any kind, he countered and destroyed the proposed new plan. His own arguments were half strategic, half psychological.

He spoke of the great distances involved, the shipping available, the extension of the present timetable, the disadvantages of invading Formosa, where the civilian population would be hostile, as opposed to the friendly Filipinos. Then he spoke of the Philippines themselves, with their "millions of wards of the American government and the thousands of American prisoners who would be left to languish in the hands of the enemy."

In MacArthur's own description of the conference to his staff later, he said:

President Roosevelt stated the general purpose of the conference was to determine the next phase of action against Japan. One plan was to attack Formosa and by-pass the Philippines. The other was to liberate the Philippines and by-pass Formosa.

Admiral Nimitz favored and presented the first plan. I favored the second, based not only on strategic but psychological grounds. Militarily, I felt and stated that, if I could secure the Philippines, it would enable us to clamp an air and naval blockade on the flow of all supplies from the south to Japan and thus, by paralyzing her industries, force her to early capitulation. Psychologically, I argued that it was not only a moral obligation to release this friendly possession from the enemy, now that it had become possible, but that to fail to do so would not be understandable to the Oriental mind.

In Japan, I held that it would be symbolical to all that Japan had failed and was doomed. Not to do so, moreover, would result in death to the thousands of prisoners, including American women, children and men civilians held in Philippine concentration camps.

To by-pass isolated islands was one thing, but to leave in your rear such a large enemy concentration, supported by an entire country's resources such as the Philippines, involved serious and unnecessary risks. I assured the President I felt confident of success if he adopted the plan.

At the conclusion of MacArthur's masterful and eloquent presentation, Roosevelt adjourned the meeting until the next morning. When the conferees had gathered again, he informed them that MacArthur's plan would prevail. He then asked the General to accompany him on a tour of the military bases near Honolulu, during which the two, according to MacArthur, "talked of other and pleasanter days," forgoing any mention of the war.

Returned to his headquarters, MacArthur told associates he was shocked at the appearance of the President and predicted, sadly, that he would not live another year. Roosevelt died just ten months later, in the first year of his fourth term. Preceding him in death was MacArthur's old friend and the godfather of his son, Manuel Quezon, first President of the Philippines. He died on August 1, 1944.

The conference at Pearl Harbor has been called by historians the most important and decisive of the war. Once it was concluded and once the decision made, Admiral Nimitz proved his own greatness by plunging wholeheartedly into efforts to make MacArthur's plan work. News correspondents assigned to his headquarters took occasion to emphasize the mutual respect with which Nimitz and MacArthur regarded each other and how effective was their co-operation. They made, it has been agreed, the most formidable Army-Navy team the world has ever seen.

And they lost no time in putting the plan into effect. On September, 1944, a massed flight of American bombers struck the port city of Davao, and Mindanao. They were the first Americans bombers the Filipinos had seen in two and a half years and they made a dramatic announcement of MacArthur's return.

The original plan of attack against the Philippines, given the code name of "Musketeer," called for an initial assault against Mindanao on November 15, followed by another against Leyte on December 20. Then, while conducting fleet air missions in support of the impending landings, Admiral "Bull" Halsey discovered that the aerial defense of Mindanao and even the islands farther north was surprisingly weak. In one of the fast changes of pace which marked the admirable flexibility of the Americans in the Pacific war, Halsey proposed attacking Leyte.

Both Nimitz and MacArthur concurred. MacArthur forwarded Halsey's proposal to the Joint Chiefs of Staff, adding that they could also move the date of the first attack up to October 20. The message was relayed to Quebec, where the Chiefs were taking part in the conference there of Churchill and Roosevelt. General Marshall's official report on the decision read:

... The message from MacArthur arrived at Quebec at night and Admiral Leahy [Chief of Staff to the President] Admiral King, General Arnold and I were being entertained at a formal dinner by Canadian officers. It was read by the appropriate staff officers who suggested an immediate affirmative answer. The message, with their recommendations, was rushed to us and we left the table for a conference. Having the utmost confidence in General MacArthur, Admiral Nimitz and Admiral Halsey, it was not a difficult decision to make.

Within ninety minutes after the signal had been received in Quebec, General MacArthur and Admiral Nimitz had received their instructions to execute the Leyte operation on the target date 20 October, abandoning the previously approved intermediary landings.

In spite of the report of Halsey's pilots, MacArthur's staff were not deceived about the resistance they could expect from the Japanese on the Philippine Islands. Many American and Philippine soldiers had escaped when Bataan fell and had been conducting well-organized guerrilla activities since. Through an almost incredibly ingenious communications system, worked out by MacArthur's intelligence officers—involving submarines, constantly changing radio codes, smuggled messages and airdrops—the strength and condition of the Japanese forces were well documented. The landing was made with the full expectation of the bitter fighting which would follow.

MacArthur left his advance headquarters at Hollandia on October 13, aboard the cruiser *Nashville,* which served as his flagship, and started the last leg of his long journey back to his second home.

Thirty-one months before, on March 11, 1942, he had left these islands in a battered PT boat, traveling by night, hiding out by day, in one of history's most famous escapes through enemy lines. Now he was returning, as he had promised—returning with an armada of six hundred and fifty battleships, aircraft carriers, cruisers, destroyers, transports and landing craft—and with a force of one hundred and fifty thousand men.

The *Nashville* zigzagged her way northward, dodging mines, wary of Japanese aircraft. On October 18, she joined the main convoy, a seemingly endless sweep of military power. At 11:00 P.M., on October 19, the General's cruiser reached her position off Leyte Gulf. The night was dark, moonless. The other ships were vague silhouettes as they rode restlessly at their assigned positions.

MacArthur was on the deck of the *Nashville* at dawn the next morning when the cruiser sliced through the waves and into the Gulf of Leyte. The big guns of the armada opened fire. As the sun cleared the horizon, he could see Tacloban, the spot where, forty-one years before, he had killed two guerrilla fighters who tried to ambush him—his baptism under fire as a young lieutenant.

He watched the first two assault waves and decided to go in with the third, taking President Sergio Osmena, Major General Basilio J. Valdes and Brigadier General Carlos Romulo of the Philippines in with him. The landing barge grounded fifty yards out. MacArthur stepped into the knee-deep water and strode ashore. A few yards away, a mobile broadcasting unit had been set up. Walking up to the mike, he spoke the message eagerly awaited by every Filipino.

"People of the Philippines: I have returned.

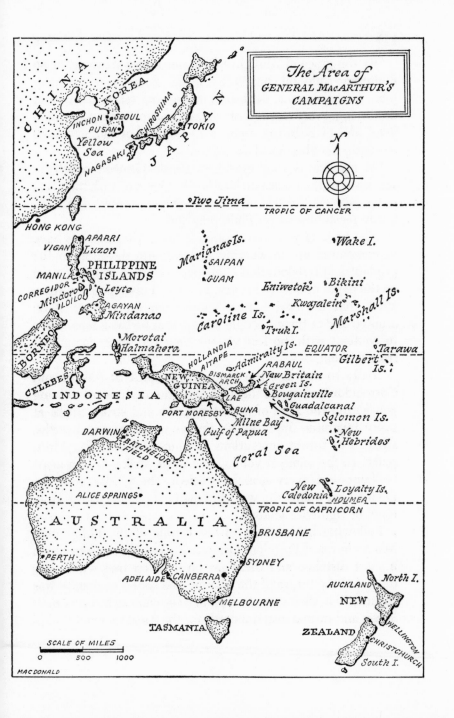

The Area of
GENERAL MacARTHUR'S
CAMPAIGNS

CHINA

KOREA
INCHON SEOUL
PUSAN
HIROSHIMA
Yellow
Sea
NAGASAKI
JAPAN
TOKIO

HONG KONG

N

Two Jima
TROPIC OF CANCER

APARRI
VIGAN Luzon
PHILIPPINE
ISLANDS
MANILA
CORREGIDOR
Mindoro
ILOILO Leyte
CAGAYAN
Mindanao

Marianas Is.
SAIPAN
GUAM

Wake I.

Eniwetok Bikini
Kwajalein
Marshall Is.
Caroline Is.
Truk I.

BORNEO

CELEBES

INDONESIA

Morotai
Halmahera

HOLLANDIA
AITAPE
NEW
GUINEA
BISMARCK
ARCH.
PORT MORESBY
LAE
BUNA
Milne Bay
Gulf of Papua

Admiralty Is.
RABAUL
New Britain
Green Is.
Bougainville
Guadalcanal
Solomon Is.

EQUATOR
Tarawa
Gilbert
Is.

New
Hebrides

DARWIN
BATCHELOR
FIELD

Coral Sea

ALICE SPRINGS

New
Caledonia
NOUMEA
Loyalty Is.

TROPIC OF CAPRICORN

AUSTRALIA

BRISBANE

PERTH

SYDNEY
ADELAIDE CANBERRA

AUCKLAND
North I.
NEW

MELBOURNE

TASMANIA

ZEALAND
WELLINGTON
CHRISTCHURCH
South I.

SCALE OF MILES
0   500   1000

MACDONALD

"By the grace of Almighty God, our forces stand again on Philippine soil—soil consecrated in the blood of our two peoples. We have come, dedicated and committed to the task of destroying every vestige of enemy control over your daily lives, and of restoring, upon a foundation of indestructible strength, the liberties of your people.

"At my side is your President, Sergio Osmena, a worthy successor of the great patriot Manuel Quezon, with members of his cabinet. The seat of your government is now, therefore, firmly reestablished on Philippine soil.

"The hour of your redemption is here. Your patriots have demonstrated an unswerving and resolute devotion to the principles of freedom that challenges the best that is written on the pages of human history. I now call upon your supreme effort that the enemy may know from the temper of an aroused and outraged people within, that he has a force there to contend with, no less violent than the force committed from without.

"Rally to me. Let the indomitable spirit of Bataan and Corregidor lead on. As the lines of battle roll forward to bring you within the zone of operations, rise and strike. Strike at every favorable opportunity. For your homes and hearths, strike. For future generations of your sons and daughters, strike. In the name of your sacred dead, strike. Let no heart be faint. Let every arm be steeled. The guidance of the Divine God points the way. Follow in the name of the Holy Grail of righteous victory."

Following his message to the People of the Philippines, MacArthur and President Osmena walked in from the beach a short distance and there sat on a fallen tree while they discussed the future of the islands. The sound of gunfire was constantly in their ears. Two palm trees were stripped of their leaves and turned into standards for the American and Philippine flags. Three days later, MacArthur restored to the Philippine government, as embodied in the duly elected President Osmena, the right to rule in that portion of Leyte which had been recaptured.

The Japanese reaction to the American landing was violent. In charge of the defense was General Tomoyuki Yamashita, who in 1942 had driven down the Malay Peninsula to Singapore. Known as the "Tiger of Malaya," Yamashita had told the British commander then, "All I want from you is a yes or no." When MacArthur invaded Leyte, Yamashita boasted that he would soon be putting the same words to the American commander.

"Yamashita is a good general," said MacArthur, when he learned of the remark, "but he talks too much."

While Yamashita was fighting to stem the wedge MacArthur's ground troops were driving into Leyte at Tacloban, and was pouring reinforcements from Luzon into the island at Ormoc (just across the island from Tacloban), the Japanese high command made a fateful decision.

To repel the invasion and maintain their position in the Philippines, they decided to commit the Japanese Combined Fleet against the American sea forces in what was to be the greatest naval battle of modern times, possibly of all times.

The ensuing struggle raged from October 23 to 26. The Japanese lost three battleships, four carriers, ten cruisers and nine destroyers. The United States lost one light carrier, two escort carriers and five other escort battlecraft.

Had the Japanese been victorious, the result would have been to leave MacArthur's forces nakedly exposed on the Philippine beaches, without air cover, reinforcements or supplies, caught between a disastrous ground and naval crossfire.

They did not succeed. The result was a decisive victory for

the American forces and it marked the end of the Japanese navy as an effective force in the war.

Although the Americans did win the battle eventually, the Japanese at one time had victory within their grasp. Only an incredible error in judgment by the Japanese commander saved the Allies. His opportunity had come about, however, due to another error, this one on the American side.

Admiral Halsey, commanding the Third Fleet, had allowed himself to be decoyed far to the north, thus leaving a major task unit of American escort carriers unguarded.

Admiral Takeo Kurita, commanding the Japanese Central Force, lay in ambush and pounced on the task unit. For two hours his superior forces inflicted terrible damage. Just as the American ships, their ammunition exhausted, were facing total destruction, Kurita inexplicably withdrew. Halsey returned shortly after that, and the day and the battle were saved. Admiral Sprague, commander of the badly mauled escort fleet, wrote, with emphasis on the last five words:

> The failure of the enemy main body and encircling light forces to completely wipe out all vessels of this Task Unit can be attributed to our successful smoke screen, our torpedo counterattack, continuous harassment of the enemy by bomb, torpedo and strafing air attacks, timely maneuvers, and the *definite partiality of Almighty God.*

On the ground, the battle of Leyte raged with vicious intensity for the next two months. The Japanese poured thousands upon thousands of reinforcements in from Luzon and they tried every trick of the jungle warfare they had learned so well. They infiltrated troops in American uniforms, they dropped parachutists in civilian clothes, they fought to the deadly, bitter end.

MacArthur had transferred his headquarters from the

cruiser *Nashville* to Tacloban before the battle for Leyte Gulf and his tan cap and corncob pipe again became a familiar sight in the forward lines of his troops. When Tacloban airstrip was cleared and Kenney sent in his fighter pilots, MacArthur was on the ground to greet them as they climbed out of their planes.

"Boy, am I glad to see you," he told them. (He had been dependent upon the Navy for fighter cover, and the recent naval battle had left that somewhat uncertain.)

The enemy had been using the port of Ormoc (since renamed MacArthur) to land his reinforcing troops. On December 7, the anniversary of Pearl Harbor, MacArthur sent the 77th Division, under Major General Andrew Bruce, for a landing at Deposito, just three and a half miles from Ormoc. The men of the 77th fought their way into Ormoc three days later, chopping the enemy up into pockets and annihilating his forces. With the fall of this port, the Japanese forces were caught in another of MacArthur's famous pincer movements, and squeezed, literally, to death.

On December 26, MacArthur reported that the campaign on Leyte was finished, except for mopping up—although this took many weeks. Figures later revealed that the Japanese had lost more than 80,000 dead—against less then 1,000 captured. Allied dead numbered 3,500, with 12,000 wounded. General Yamashita had lost the greatest battle in Japanese army history.

With the capture of Leyte, MacArthur was awarded the Philippine Medal of Valor, that nation's highest award. The United States promoted him to the five-star rank of General of the Army, America's highest present rank.

His next move was to take another step toward Luzon and the Philippine capital of Manila. The island of Mindoro had been selected and landing operations had already been accomplished there, without the loss of a single man. By December 23, two air strips on Mindoro were ready for operation, and MacArthur was ready for Luzon.

On January 8, 1943, in the light cruiser *Boise*, MacArthur led his landing force into Lingayen Gulf, on the northwest coast of Luzon, where, three years before, General Homma's transports had sent the Japanese invaders ashore to commence the battle for Bataan and Corregidor. On the way to the Gulf, his ship had been the target for a submarine's torpedo, which it evaded, and for two *kamikaze* attacks, which barely missed. MacArthur watched all three from the deck of the *Boise*, calmly smoking his corncob pipe.

Other ships of the invasion fleet were not so fortunate. The Japanese resorted to *kamikaze* during the last stages of the war and did enormous damage to naval craft. It was the most direct form of attack and almost impossible to stop. The Japanese suicide pilots simply turned their aircraft into guided missiles and flew them onto the decks of the allied ships, exploding on impact!

Going into Lingayen, the escort carrier *Ommaney Bay* was so badly damaged she had to be sunk. Half a dozen destroyers were hit, as well as the cruiser *Columbia* and the battleship *New Mexico*.

At 9:30 on the morning of January 9, MacArthur watched the first assault waves hit the beaches of Lingayen. Threatened landings at Legaspi, Batangas and other southern Luzon ports had sent the bulk of the Japanese forces in this direction and the main attack at Lingayen again caught the enemy by surprise.

Meantime, the guerrillas, acting under MacArthur's orders, had been active. They had prepared detailed maps where enemy arms and fuel were stored. They cut enemy supply

Douglas MacArthur   163

and communication lines, ambushed patrols and destroyed
supply dumps.

As General MacArthur wrote: "Their shining bolos turned
red." His staff estimated that the guerrilla forces on Luzon
alone did the work of a complete division.

Backing slowly from Lingayen, the Japanese resisted desperately. They had had time to fortify their position. Buried
tanks served as pillboxes. As usual, they never surrendered.
It took the Allies twelve days to reach Tarlac, in the central
plains, halfway to Manila.

Here the Japanese launched a savage attack and the allied
lines faltered and gave ground. MacArthur reached the scene
as the defending 161st Division was getting its breath and,
with its field commanders, led a counterattack which all but
annihilated the Japanese in front of them. MacArthur was
awarded his third Distinguished Service Cross.

February saw the United States Eleventh Corps landing
(without the loss of a man) on the western Zimbales coast,
at Olongapo. By mid-month, they were sitting astride the
entrance to Bataan and moved in to cover the entrance to
Manila Bay. Clark Field fell to the Fourteenth Corps and the
gateway to Manila itself was open.

MacArthur, as he afterward wrote, was "fighting on hal-
lowed ground." It was the same soil which had seen his
father's triumphs at the turn of the century. MacArthur himself had campaigned over every foot of it and this great
familiarity enabled him to avoid many a pitfall, escape many
a trap and save the lives of many men. He was constantly in
the front lines, liable to bob up, with his tan cap and corncob pipe, at any hour and any place.

General Kenney and other writers (including MacArthur)
tell the story of an incident that took place near Tarlac. Kenney had dropped into MacArthur's advance headquarters to

report. They were having dinner and Kenney noticed Mac-
Arthur was scarcely touching his food. He inquired about it.

"George," said MacArthur, "I'm so darn tired I can't eat."

As Kenney was preparing to leave before daybreak the
next morning, he told the duty officer to inform MacArthur
he regretted that he could not delay to say good-by.

"Oh," said the duty officer, "General MacArthur left for
the front two hours ago."

MacArthur entered Manila with the advance troops on
February 3, in time to see his old home atop the Manila hotel
fired by the retreating Japanese. His entrance was a sign for
a celebration which reached near-hysteria wherever he appeared. The liberated Philippine people clung to his arms,
kissed his hands and wept with joy. He refused to have any
formal ceremony.

One of the factors uppermost in his mind as he began the
fight across Luzon was the fate of the thousands of Americans and Filipinos, civilians and military, that the Japanese
had herded into concentration camps three years before. His
first attention at every point was to get help to these prisoners before the Japanese had time to—as he feared might happen—do away with them completely. He organized a daring
liberation for one camp and reached others in time to save
the virtually starving inmates.

At Bilibid, he found the tattered, emaciated remnants of
the men who had fought on Bataan and Corregidor. He
walked down the line of cots, where the men tried to stand
at attention, with tears streaming down his face as they
whispered the words—"You made it," and sometimes just,
"God bless you."

He could only reply, "I'm long overdue, long overdue."

Corregidor fell on February 16, 1945, under four thousand
tons of bombs from Kenney's airmen and a landing of 2,065

paratroopers. Some six thousand Japanese surrendered. For his own return to the island, MacArthur gathered up the men who had accompanied him on the flight from the island three years before. In four PT boats, borrowed from the Navy, they pulled up to the same old dock, but this time in broad daylight. He directed that the colors be hoisted on the old flagpole. He told the assembled officers and men:

Bataan, with Corregidor the citadel of its integral defense, made possible all that has happened here. History, I am sure, will record it as one of the decisive battles of the world. Its long-protracted struggle enabled the Allies to gather strength to resist in the Pacific. Had it not held out, Australia would have fallen, with incalculably disastrous results.

Our triumphs today belong equally to that dead army [of Bataan and Corregidor]. Its heroism and sacrifice have been fully acclaimed but the great strategic results of that mighty defense are only now becoming fully apparent. The Bataan garrison was destroyed, due to its dreadful handicaps, but no army in history more thoroughly accomplished its mission. Let no man henceforth speak of it other than as of a magnificent victory.

On July 4, MacArthur announced the end of the Philippine campaign—and was cited for his fourth Distinguished Service Medal. He felt the end of the war was very near.

14

O N APRIL 3, 1945, a reorganization of the Pacific Theater
command structure was authorized. MacArthur was
designated commander-in-chief of all U.S. Army forces. Nimitz was placed in command of Navy forces. The Twentieth
Air Force, newly equipped with the Boeing Superfortresses
which the Japanese called the "Whispering Death," was being run direct from Washington by General Henry A. "Hap"
Arnold.

All three officers, incidentally, carried five-star rank. Mac-
Arthur had been promoted to be General of the Army on December 18, 1944. Nimitz was named Admiral of the Fleet on
December 19, and Arnold a General of the Army on December 21. (Later, when the Air Force became a separate service, Arnold's title was changed to General of the Air Force.)

Well before the last Japanese stragglers were driven out of
the Philippines, MacArthur was asked by Washington to
submit plans for a final assault against Japan to end the war.
He proposed three possible courses of action, but recommended one. It was, as quoted in official records:

To attack the southern island of Kyushu, installing sufficient air
forces there to cover a subsequent assault on Honshu, the heart

of Japan. This course would attain neutralization by placing our air power at the closest practicable distance from the final objective in Japan; it would permit application of full power of our combined resources, ground, naval and air, on that objective.

I am of the opinion that the combined resources in the Pacific are adequate to carry out the course. The Japanese Fleet has been reduced to practical impotency. Its attrition is heavy and its power for sustained action is diminishing rapidly.

The Joint Chiefs of Staff in Washington approved the plan and on May 5, issued the necesary directives. Code name of the overall operation was "Downfall." The first phase, the landing on Kyushu, was called "Olympic" and the final assault on Honshu was given the name of "Coronet." The target date for launching the operation was November 1, 1945.

Meantime, the war moved on in other parts of the world. On April 18, 1945, underground fighters caught Mussolini trying to escape to Switzerland and executed him. Hitler committed suicide in his Berlin bunker the night of April 29-30. On May 7 the German nation surrendered.

In the Pacific Theater and apart from MacArthur's operations, the American Marines took Iwo Jima in March, 1945—producing, incidentally, one of the greatest picture scenes of the war: that of the Marines raising the American flag over the island, now cast into a famous Marine memorial. Okinawa fell in April, after eighty-three days of fighting in which the Japanese lost one hundred and ten thousand men.

At the Potsdam Conference, in which President Truman replaced the late President Roosevelt as one of the "Big Three," with Churchill and Stalin, the Allies gave Japan the ultimatum of unconditional surrender. To emphasize the force back of the stipulation, air and navy offensives against Japan were stepped up. Flying out of the Mariana Islands (chiefly Guam), the Air Force averaged some twelve hundred sorties (each plane in a flight counts as one sortie) a week. The Third Fleet sailed the Japanese waters unmolested, shelling coastal cities.

Then, on August 7, President Truman startled and shocked the world with the famous broadcast which said:

Sixteen hours ago, an American airplane dropped one bomb on Hiroshima. That single bomb had more power than twenty thousand tons of explosive. It is an atomic bomb. It is a harnessing of the basic power of the universe. We are now preparing to obliterate more rapidly and completely every productive enterprise the Japanese have above ground in any city.

The Soviet government declared war against Japan the next day, having observed a scrupulous neutrality for four years. For Stalin it was the chance to share in a cheap victory.

On August 9, the second of the only two atomic bombs ever unleashed in anger struck Nagasaki. One hundred thousand people died in a matter of seconds. (This second bomb was dropped on Nagasaki through an accident of weather. The original target had been the city of Kokura. On August 9, Kokura was covered by clouds and the alternate target of Nagasaki was chosen instead.)

The Japanese notified the Allies, through its Minister in neutral Switzerland, that it was ready to accept the ultimatum of unconditional surrender. With the concurrence of other governments concerned, General MacArthur was designated "Supreme Commander of the Allied Powers" (SCAP) to administer and accept the surrender.

After an interchange of messages between Manila and Tokyo, MacArthur directed the Japanese government to send to Manila "a competent representative empowered to receive in the name of the Emperor, the Japanese government and the Japanese General Headquarters, certain requirements for carrying into effect the terms of surrender."

A delegation was duly sent, headed by Lieutenant General Torashiro Kawabe, vice chief of the Imperial General Staff. With fifteen staff members, he arrived in Manila on August 19, and the party was taken to MacArthur's headquarters.

The reception accorded them was coldly austere. For the flight into Allied territory the Japanese were told to use the radio recognition letters "BATAAN." The Japanese replied suggesting "JNP" instead. The instructions were repeated. "BATAAN" it was.

MacArthur pointedly did not attend the conference. The Japanese officers were required to leave their ceremonial swords in the reception room. MacArthur's instructions and directives to them, translated into Japanese, were clear and complete. General Kawabe was never asked for an opinion or a suggestion. He was told. Among other requirements, his instructions were to:

Repair Atsugi airfield, near Yokohama, for the arrival of MacArthur's party.
Remove the propellers from all the Japanese aircraft on Atsugi.
Remove any armed troops from the Tokyo area.
Provide transportation into Yokohama.
Clear Yokohama's Grand Hotel for MacArthur's party.

The one protest from the party was as to whether or not they would be able to repair Atsugi. This was not accepted, and MacArthur's staff did not learn until later the real reason for it. Atsugi was the headquarters and training base for the *kamikaze* pilots. Many of them had been on the base, awaiting their final missions, and were still there. Some had received the solemn last rites of the dead. They had not only refused to surrender but broke into the palace grounds in search of the Emperor (an unheard-of sacrilege), killed the commanding general of the Imperial Guard and set fire to the home of the Prime Minister before being subdued. General

Kawabe had his own worries that they might not remain subdued.

Advance communications units from MacArthur's headquarters arrived at Atsugi on August 28. They were followed by troop transports carrying some four thousand men of the 11th Airborne Division. It was a casual, almost contemptuous show of strength in an enemy country which still had more than two million men under arms. General Robert Eichelberger, MacArthur's ground commander, landed the morning of August 30, to inspect the field and arrangements.

Then, at two that afternoon, MacArthur's C-54 with "Bataan" emblazoned on its side, circled the field, landed and taxied into position. The door opened and MacArthur stood there a moment, surveying the scene, listening to the music of the 11th Airborne's band, shirt open at the throat, tan cap and corncob pipe in place. He might have been standing on his own front porch. Greeting Eichelberger, he said, "Bob, this is the payoff, as they say in the movies."

The cars in the motor convoy lined up to take MacArthur into the city were old and road-worn, the best the Japanese could muster. Leading the procession was, unbelievably, an ancient fire engine.

MacArthur climbed into the first auto, an oldish Lincoln. Members of his staff sorted themselves out in the cars behind. The procession started for Yokohama.

The order of dress for MacArthur's staff that day had originally included sidearms. MacArthur saw it and said: "We will go unarmed."

Now, as the motorcade moved toward the city, it passed between the lines of two armed Japanese army divisions, thirty thousand men, lining each side of the road, facing outward. Days before, Douglas MacArthur was the greatest of the enemy. This day, while their backs were turned in perhaps respect, perhaps sadness, they were watching the crowd to protect the silent impassive General who, more than any other man, had conquered them. His safety was a fine point of national honor and MacArthur had correctly interpreted their feelings.

Years later, Winston Churchill said, "Of all the amazing deeds of personal bravery of the war, I regard MacArthur's personal landing at Atsugi as the greatest of the lot."

The next day, immersed in the details of arranging the surrender ceremony which was to take place aboard the battleship *Missouri*, MacArthur received word that General Jonathan Wainwright, leader of the Bataan forces, and General Sir Arthur E. Percival, British commander at Singapore, had been freed from their prison camp near Mukden and had reached Manila. He immediately ordered them flown to Yokohama, so they could take part in the next day's surrender signing.

MacArthur met Wainwright in his quarters at the Grand Hotel that night. An associate described the scene:

General Wainwright never deserved the nickname "Skinny" more than he did then. Somewhere he had found a new uniform, but it hung in folds. He seemed to have aged twenty years. He leaned on a cane as he walked. His cheeks were sunken and his neck scrawny. His head seemed too big for his body.

MacArthur put both arms about him and could only whisper "Jim—Jim." It was a personal name that only he used for Wainwright. The two men talked for hours over dinner.

The formal ceremony attending Japan's surrender took place on September 2, 1945, on the deck of Admiral Halsey's Third Fleet flagship, the U.S.S. *Missouri*. It was a misty Sunday morning and the sky was lightly clouded. The deck was crowded with representatives of various nations which had fought in the Pacific. Motion picture cameramen perched on a platform built for the purpose. News correspondents held down a dozen vantage points.

MacArthur arrived at 8:45 and immediately went to Halsey's cabin. A few minutes later, the Japanese delegation came alongside in a small launch. Leading the group was Foreign Minister Namoru Shigemitsu, whose high silk hat and frock coat contrasted strangely with the military uniforms. Behind him came General Yoshijiro Umezu of the Imperial General Staff, and nine other Japanese representatives. Shigemitsu had trouble negotiating the ship's ladder with the artificial leg he wore, the result of a bomb explosion.

MacArthur let the Japanese wait, as one of their members wrote years later, "like penitent boys awaiting the dreaded schoolmaster," for many minutes before he came out with Nimitz and Halsey. He made a brief statement, concluding:

"It is my earnest hope that from this solemn occasion a better world shall emerge—a world dedicated to the dignity of man. The terms and conditions upon which surrender of the Japanese Imperial forces is here to be given and accepted are contained in the instrument of surrender before you."

He beckoned to Shigemitsu, who signed twice, once in the English version and again in the Japanese. Umezu signed for the Japanese Army.

When they had finished signing, MacArthur signaled to Generals Wainwright and Percival, and the two men so recently released from prison camp stood behind him as he signed. MacArthur used five pens for his signature. One each went to Percival and Wainwright. A small red pen was Jean MacArthur's. The fourth went to President Truman, and the last MacArthur kept.

The other nations signed in turn—China, the United Kingdom, Russia, Australia, Canada, France, the Netherlands and New Zealand. The Japanese received their copy. MacArthur said: "The ceremony is finished." He arose and left the table. The Japanese bowed stiffly and departed. The signing had taken twenty minutes.

That night, MacArthur broadcast a message to the people of the United States from the deck of the *Missouri:*

"Today the guns are silent. A great tragedy has ended. A great victory has been won. The skies no longer rain death—the seas bear only commerce—men everywhere walk upright in the sunlight. The entire world is quietly at peace. The holy mission has been completed. And in reporting this to you, the people, I speak for the thousands of silent lips, forever stilled among the jungles and the beaches and in the deep waters of the Pacific which marked the way. I speak for the unnamed brave millions homeward bound to take up the challenge of that future which they did so much to salvage from the brink of disaster.

"As I look back on the long, tortuous trail from those grim days of Bataan and Corregidor, when an entire world lived in fear; when democracy was on the defensive everywhere; when modern civilization trembled in the balance, I thank a merciful God that He has given us the faith, the courage and the power from which to mold victory. We have known the bitterness of defeat and the exultation of triumph, and from both we have learned there can be no turning back. We must go forward to preserve in peace what we won in war."

15

☆ ☆ ☆ ☆ ☆

W HEN MacArthur assumed his duties as Supreme Commander of the Allied Powers, in September, 1945, his
authority over the Japanese was essentially absolute. His
directive from the Four Powers—United States, Great Britain,
Soviet Union and China—read:

From the moment of surrender, the authority of the Emperor
and the Japanese government to rule the state will be subject to
you and you will take such steps as you deem proper to effectuate
the surrender terms. You will exercise supreme command over all
land, sea and air forces which may be allocated for enforcement
in Japan of the surrender terms by the Allied forces concerned.

As the virtual dictator of a nation of eighty million people,
Douglas MacArthur could have been vengeful. Instead, he
was benevolent.

Japan, up until the political and spiritual changes wrought
by the occupation, was a curious mixture of the twentieth
century and medieval feudalism. The country was ruled by
an Emperor who reigned with absolute power by the divine
right of his supposed descent from the Sun Goddess. Civil
rights, freedom of action, even of thought, were unknown to
the peasant masses. (In the three years preceding the war,

the *Kempei-Tai,* or secret police, had arrested more than fifty thousand persons for "dangerous thinking.")

During the war, the Japanese people, military and civilian alike, had been subjected to never-ending barrages of words and cartoons depicting the Allies—and particularly the Americans—as inhuman, cruel, brutal. And MacArthur was caricatured as the most bestial of the lot.

Prepared as they were for the worst, the opening days of the occupation came as something of a shock to the Japanese. The American troops scattered out over the islands of the Japanese homeland. The Emperor's armies had traditionally, when victorious, lived off the conquered lands with no particular thought to the starving population. Under MacArthur's orders, the occupation forces not only furnished their own food and supplies but they brought in thousands of tons to supplement the produce of the ravaged country. A few days after the surrender, twenty truckloads of flour, canned goods and rice arrived in Yokosuka (near Yokohama) for the relief of the local population—(to the amazement of the mayor.) Medical supplies, blankets and tea followed. Throughout the country, American soldiers were delighted by Japanese children. They gave them candy and chocolate bars and taught them the dubious art of chewing gum. The first week of the occupation, an injured child was rushed by American jeep to an American hospital for treatment in one of a score of human incidents. Reasonable fraternization was permitted, as reflected in the statistics of the thousands of pretty Japanese girls who came to America later as war brides. Gradually, the picture of the American soldier changed, in the eyes of the Japanese, from a beastlike conqueror to a somewhat boyish, generous and friendly person.

After the surrender ceremony, MacArthur moved immediately to Tokyo, where he took up residence in the American

Embassy. It had escaped serious damage during the aerial bombings, but had lain idle for many years and needed complete refurbishing. Once made livable, MacArthur immediately brought Jean MacArthur, little Arthur, Ah Cheu and Arthur's tutor, Mrs. Phyllis Gibbons, from Manila and restored his own home life.

The Embassy had been built during the Hoover administration as a show place. The compound surrounding it was enclosed, with big gates flanking the living quarters, known as the "big house," which sat atop a small hill. Behind this, a winding path led to a swimming pool, smaller reflecting pools and a formal garden. Two other buildings were divided into apartments for guests and the Embassy staff. On the grounds, but accessible through another gate, was the chancery.

With the repairs to the buildings, the cleaning of the pool, the planting and trimming of shrubs completed, the old Embassy staff returned, without summons or invitation. One by one, they appeared, announced themselves and took up their duties.

With his personal household in place and under the competent supervision of his wife, MacArthur settled himself into the routine which was never to vary during his entire stay there, until he left in 1951.

The General's day began about 7:30, when he would arise. Jean MacArthur usually joined him in his bedroom for the morning's first cup of coffee. He invariably wore an old gray dressing gown, adorned with his West Point "A." Promptly at eight, the three MacArthur dogs, Brownie, Blackie and Yuki, with young Arthur, invaded the bedroom for a wild romp. Family prayers, led by Mrs. Gibbons, were followed by family breakfast, usually fruit, cereal, eggs and coffee. At eight-thirty Arthur was borne off to start the day's school and General MacArthur's work began.

Dispatches and messages which had accumulated during the night had been brought to his quarters and he went through them swiftly. Aides at the office scanned and sorted out the news from wire service tickers and telephoned him anything of importance—including football scores in the fall, with particular attention to items concerning West Point.

At ten-thirty on the minute, the General appeared at the Embassy door and stepped into his car, a black Cadillac, which moved down the shrub-lined driveway. Two sentries at the gate presented arms. MacArthur returned the salutes. He nodded to the Japanese policemen in their police box across the street. At each intersection, the Japanese traffic policemen noted his approach and directed him through with no change of pace. The route continued past Japan's Finance Building, the bomb-ruined Navy Building, past the Sakurada Gate of the Imperial Palace and up to the six-story Dai Ichi (Number One) Building. Another two sentries came to present arms as the General stepped from the car. He returned their salutes and nodded to the bowing crowd that was invariably there—when he left and when he entered. Striding into the building, he stepped into a waiting elevator and rode to the sixth floor.

The trip from the Embassy to Dai Ichi always took exactly ten minutes. Its route never varied, nor its pace. In the beginning, MacArthur's staff had placed a jeep with guards ahead and another behind his limousine. When he stopped that—and after the Cadillac once broke down en route—the staff had him more discreetly followed at a distance of two blocks by guards in fatigue clothes. MacArthur never knew this.

His office in the Dai Ichi Building was walnut-paneled, air-conditioned and large. His desk was covered in green baize and notably unadorned with the usual desk gadgetry. There was a rack for his pipes, a bowl of tobacco, a letter opener, pencils, two letter trays, one marked "in" and the other "out." There was no telephone. On the rare occasions when it was necessary to receive a call, the General took it in one of the adjoining offices. He had no secretary. Most of his letters he wrote in longhand on a yellow pad and they were typed by one of the pool typists.

In the leather chair behind his desk, MacArthur attacked two piles of business always ready for him. One was the morning's business, the other mail addressed to him personally. The envelopes of the latter were slit partly open, but not all the way. Reading and making his decisions quickly, MacArthur placed the business to be handled by other offices in one stack, the mail he would answer himself in another. Some he would handle immediately, the rest put aside until later in the day. It was a rigid rule of the headquarters that all business must be taken care of, as far as possible, on the day it arrived.

The rest of the morning brought visitors on a tight schedule —Japanese officials or visiting personalities and delegations, usually from the United States. MacArthur was unfailingly relaxed for his guests. He listened with interest. Usually briefed in advance by his staff and with his own wide field of knowledge, he could and did ask penetrating questions and frequently disconcerted his visitors by his grasp and insight of the subject under discussion. No one ever left MacArthur's office with the impression that he hadn't received an appreciative audience.

If there were to be guests at lunch, MacArthur tried to be at the Embassy by one-thirty. If not, he might be in the office as late as two in the afternoon and, on those days, the crowd of Japanese waiting for him to appear had reached well into the street. The salutes to the sentries, the nods to the crowd, the path to the Embassy followed the pattern of the morning.

Lunch was informal, with MacArthur at one end of the table and Jean MacArthur at the other and no prearranged seating, except for the guest of honor at the host's right. There were no cocktails, and lunch started promptly when the General arrived. The menu was unelaborate—soup, a meat, two vegetables, salad, ice cream and cookies, and coffee. The meal might last two hours and more, particularly if MacArthur was being drawn out on a subject on which he felt strongly. If the group did not linger too long over coffee and cigars, the General would have a nap. If it was late, he returned to his office immediately, where the morning's routine was repeated until seven, usually, but sometimes as late as ten at night. Back in his Embassy quarters and after a light dinner, MacArthur's love of movies took over. There was invariably a film ready each evening. The family, the staff, even the sentries joined in watching.

MacArthur rarely did anything by chance and it was not by chance that he adopted a deliberate policy of remoteness in his position. He felt this "ivory tower" attitude and almost ghostlike figure of the Supreme Commander would both awe and impress the Japanese. It did. On his arrival in Tokyo, he made the required courtesy calls to the Embassies of the other powers. Thereafter, he never attended a function or a party. When it seemed essential that a MacArthur be present, Jean went. Although he frequently had guests for luncheon, he never entertained at dinner or in the evening. Tokyo never saw him except on that well-worn path between the Embassy and the Dai Ichi Building, four times a day, seven days a week. He took no trips, no vacations, no days off. He attended no public functions, no athletic contests, no entertainments, visited no show places. When two months had passed and he had not called on the Emperor, the Emperor called on him. Alone (although Jean MacArthur peeked down the stairway), except for an interpreter, they talked for two hours but neither ever mentioned about what.

MacArthur's program to impress the Japanese people as to his own personality (which succeeded remarkably) was only one small side of his activities. Facing him was the incredibly complex task—for him a crusade—of bringing the Japanese nation and people out of the darkness of feudalism and into the light of modern freedom and dignity.

He did not delay the start. Only thirty-two days after the surrender, he issued a set of orders which became known as his "Civil Liberties Directive." It abolished the Kempei-Tai secret police, released all political prisoners, suspended all existing laws restricting political, civil and religious liberties and gave women the vote. Simultaneously, he gently pushed the Japanese Diet (Congress) into writing a new and liberal election law and then called for a general election to be held seven months ahead, on April 10, 1946.

Almost always the velvet glove was sufficient; when it was not, MacArthur had no hesitation in using the iron hand for what he considered a good cause.

Implementing the terms of the surrender document, Mac-Arthur directed that all persons who had actively engaged in militaristic and ultra-nationalistic activities prior to the war should be removed from public office. This included several ministers in the cabinet of Prime Minister Shidehara. Misinterpreting MacArthur's usual gentle methods, the cabinet decided to resign en masse in protest. It was planned, as announced to the press, that their resignations would be handed to the Emperor (as called for by the then-unchanged

Japanese constitution), who would then ask Shidehara to form a new cabinet. Officially informed of the action, MacArthur told his informant, the Foreign Minister:

"Mr. Minister, I have the highest regard for Baron Shidehara, and I know of no one better qualified to carry out the terms of my directive, but if the cabinet resigns en masse tomorrow, it can only be interpreted by the Japanese people that it is unable to implement my directive. Thereafter, Baron Shidehara may be acceptable to the Emperor for reappointment as Prime Minister, but he will not be acceptable to me."

Only those cabinet members disqualified by MacArthur's decree resigned.

It was imperative that a new constitution be written and available so that the Japanese people could vote on it in the April election. In October of 1945, a committee of Japanese political leaders was named to prepare a draft. Three months later, they submitted to MacArthur a barely reworded revision of the old constitution. After further hedging and delays by the politicos, and when it became apparent they would not or could not produce an acceptable document, MacArthur dismissed their efforts, selected the best American constitutional experts available and instructed them to draft a constitution embodying the best factors of the democratic constitutions of the world. The resulting document was accepted on February 22, Washington's Birthday, partly due to the surprising enthusiasm of the Emperor himself, although it stripped him of the ancient divine powers, as well as vast properties.

The new constitution was published widely, so that the Japanese people would have the opportunity to study it. In the April election, they approved its adoption overwhelmingly. In that election, incidentally, three-fourths of the eligible electorate (thirteen million of them women) went to the polls for the first free election ever held in Japan. The Diet they elected held only six "old-line" politicians. The others were educators, authors, physicians and farmers. Thirty-eight of the elected were women.

These actions were followed in reasonably rapid order by a new economic program, tax revision, a new national financial structure, new labor laws permitting unionization, an educational program with millions of new textbooks which deleted military and other propaganda, and by the implementation of freedom in religious worship.

In 1945, Japan was twenty years and more behind the western nations in medicine and particularly in public health programs. Epidemics of cholera, diphtheria, typhoid and smallpox were common, and tuberculosis was endemic to the population. MacArthur was instrumental in setting up a Ministry of Public Health and Welfare within the cabinet and the greatest mass inoculations in history were carried out.

Throughout many generations the arable land of Japan had been owned by the feudal lords of the country. In 1945, more than half of these lands were worked by sharecroppers under an exorbitant system of rents. At MacArthur's urging, the Diet passed laws enabling the government to purchase much of this land and then sell to the small farmers on long-term credit. Almost five million acres were transferred as a result.

The MacArthur rule in Japan—and rule it was—is unique and unparalleled in history. As the virtual dictator over a nation of defeated but resourceful people, this wise and gifted man seized the opportunity to create a new nation which, in the structure of its government and civil appurtenances, embodied the best that existed in the modern world. His was a situation of which ambitious men dream; it was also a situation with which not all men could have been trusted. Mac-

Arthur accomplished a monumental task, certainly with competent help which he sought constantly. He accomplished it with pride but with no sense of personal gain except his own already secure place in world history.

16

☆ ☆ ☆ ☆ ☆

THE LAST chapter of General Douglas MacArthur's military career opened on Sunday morning, June 25, 1950. He was awakened by the jangling bell of the telephone by his bed and, lifting the receiver in the pre-dawn darkness, he heard the duty officer say:

"General, I am sorry to disturb you at this early hour, but we have just received a dispatch from Seoul, advising that the North Koreans have struck in great strength south across the 38th parallel at four o'clock this morning."

At the end of the war in the Pacific, Korea had been divided at the 38th parallel. The northern half was Communist. The southern half, under American occupation, had been formed into a democracy, the Republic of Korea, with Syngman Rhee serving as president. The American occupation had ended in 1948 and MacArthur's only present responsibility there was to evacuate some two thousand Americans in case of disaster.

Later that day, at the request of the United States, a special meeting of the United Nations Security Council passed a resolution which charged that the action of the North Korean forces constituted a breach of the peace and:

1. Called for immediate cessation of hostilities for the North Koreans to withdraw back of the 38th parallel;

2. Requested that the United Nations Temporary Commission on Korea (previously appointed to help guide South Korea) communicate its recommendations on the situation, observe the North Korean withdrawal and advise the Security Council of compliance with the resolution;

3. Called upon all members of the United Nations to render every assistance to the United Nations in the execution of the resolution and to refrain from giving assistance to the North Korean authorities.

The resolution went through the Security Council without a veto, primarily because the Russians were temporarily boycotting the United Nations. President Truman interpreted the phrase "render every assistance" as an authorization to help the South Koreans militarily. American forces were, in fact, already committed. On June 26, American aircraft had driven off enemy fighter planes threatening the evacuation of American nationals, which, incidentally, was carried out without loss or injury.

On June 27, the United Nations passed a second resolution, calling on all members to give military assistance to South Korea to repel the invaders. That same day, MacArthur was named United Nations Commander. The American Seventh Fleet and the British Naval forces in the area were placed under his command.

On June 28, he invited four news correspondents to his office, informed them he was going to fly to the Korean front the next day and offered to take them along. His plane, *Bataan*, he told them, would be unarmed. There was no assurance of fighter cover.

"If you are not at the airport tomorrow," he said, "I will understand that you have other commitments." Amused by their protests that of course they would be there, he told them, "I have no doubt of your courage, gentlemen. I just wanted to give your judgment time to work."

The military situation in Korea was both chaotic and disheartening. The South Koreans had four divisions defending the 38th parallel. They had been trained and armed as constabulary troops and were equipped mainly with rifles and machine guns. Against these thirty-five to forty thousand lightly armed men, the North Koreans threw sixty thousand troops of the line, fully equipped with artillery and Soviet-made tanks.

At his office in Dai Ichi Building and in his Embassy home, MacArthur smoked the classical, straight-stemmed briar pipes. As the *Bataan* splashed away from the runway at Tokyo's Haneda Airport, he pulled out the old familiar corn-cob. The tan cap was in place, with its malevolent-eyed eagle glaring defiance. His shirt was open at the throat. There was a war on; he was commanding.

The *Bataan* picked up four Mustang fighters as escort at the Japanese coastline and, over Korea, they drove off a Russian-built Yak fighter. The *Bataan* landed at Suwon, below Inchon on the west coast, where MacArthur listened to a briefing from a military advisory group in their headquarters, a schoolhouse.

Then he said, "Let's take a look at the front."

The "front" at this time was as fluid and uncertain as rising flood waters. Tank-led North Korean spearheads were slicing through the South Korean lines almost at will. Suwon and the neighboring roads were being strafed regularly. Two ruined transport planes just off the runways were smoldering testimony to the accuracy of enemy bombing. (The *Bataan* had been sent back to Tokyo with orders to return at five o'clock.)

In an old sedan and accompanying jeeps, the MacArthur party took off northward to the Han River, moving slowly through what MacArthur described as "the backwash of a defeated, disorganized army." Mingled with the retreating troops were the streaming refugees, frightened and silent but not hysterical. Men carried salvaged household belongings, women led and carried children, wide-eyed but tearless. The desolation and rubble of the battlefield already lay in the surrounding fields, along with the dead.

The General's party reached the Han in time to watch, only yards away, the last rear-guard action defending and destroying the bridges. Across the Han, and only a mile away, they could see the South Korean capital of Seoul. It had just been captured. The smoke of bomb and artillery fires rose between the turrets of buildings dating back to the fourteenth century.

MacArthur walked up to the crest of a small hill where he stood for many minutes, watching the fighting below . . . then he turned for the trip back to the airfield. He thought of Bataan and Corregidor, of New Guinea and Buna. Once again, he was confronted with a desperate situation and ordered to save it with pitifully small resources. But on the hilltop he had determined his strategy.

On the return trip, the little motor convoy was attacked by fighter planes. Everyone dived for the ditches—with one exception. The others looked back to see MacArthur by the side of the road, erect, hands on hips, corncob pipe in mouth, watching as the planes strafed the highway. One jeep was knocked out of commission, others were hit.

In Tokyo, the United Nations Commander moved with characteristic swiftness and decision. First of all, he must stop the enemy's headlong rush. There was grave danger that its momentum, if not immediately checked, would carry it across the peninsula and to the sea. All of Korea would then be lost. Available in Japan he had four American divisions of occupation troops, all woefully understrength, and a battalion of Australians.

His first move was—in his own words—"an arrogant display of strength." He sent two rifle companies and a mortar platoon, some five hundred men, to Korea by air, with orders to establish road blocks and harass the enemy. They moved into action near Suwon, which the North Koreans had taken, and in one of the most gallant actions of any war, engaged the enemy at twenty-to-one odds.

The little force was virtually annihilated, but it accomplished its purpose and saved Korea. When the North Korean commander came up against the Americans, he hesitated. He had known the strength and armament of the South Koreans. What the American force might be, how large and how strong, he did not know. Unwilling to take a chance, he stopped his drive, regrouped his units and stabilized his lines. By that time, his golden opportunity was gone. MacArthur had gained ten precious days to move two divisions to Korea and to form them into the Eighth Army under General Walton Walker.

A few weeks later, when his pleas for reinforcements were turned down by Washington (a decision which is difficult to understand from this distance in time), he integrated the remaining divisions of the South Korean Army into the American units through the use of the "buddy system"—one Korean, one American. After some early misunderstandings, the "buddy system" worked beyond all hopes. Each man had what the other lacked, the Americans a knowledge of the weapons used, the Koreans a knowledge of the terrain and the enemy. Both had courage.

By mid-July, some twenty days after the North Korean

invasion, the United Nations defense was well on the way to being stabilized into what was known as the Pusan Perimeter. MacArthur was able to report to President Truman:

Our hold upon the southern part of Korea represents a secure base. Our casualties, despite overwhelming odds, have been relatively light. Our strength will continually increase, while that of the enemy will relatively decrease. His supply line is insecure. He had his great chance and failed to exploit it. We are now in Korea in force and, with God's help, we are there to stay *until* the constitutional authority of the Republic is fully restored.

MacArthur might have added that he was now ready to take the initiative. In other messages to the Joint Chiefs of Staff, he had proposed an amphibious landing at the South Korean port of Inchon, on the west coast near the capital of Seoul. He told them:

"Operation planned mid-September is amphibious landing of two-division corps in rear of enemy lines for purpose of enveloping and destroying enemy forces in conjunction with attack from south by Eighth Army. I am firmly convinced that early and strong effort behind his front will sever his main lines of communication and enable us to deliver a decisive and crushing blow.

"The alternative," he added, "is a frontal attack which can only result in a protracted and expensive campaign."

In mid-August, MacArthur was informed that General Lawton Collins, Army Chief of Staff, and Admiral Forrest Sherman, Chief of Naval Operations, were en route to discuss the Inchon maneuver. And at five-thirty on the evening of August 23, 1950, the conference began. In addition to MacArthur, Collins and Sherman, a number of high-ranking officers of the Marines and the Air Force were present.

As in another conference at Pearl Harbor in 1944, the Navy

took the floor first. Their presentation was logical. Inchon, said the Navy, on the date set for the invasion, would have a tidal rise and fall of thirty feet, one of the greatest in the world. At high tide, the current raced and churned through the port entry, "Flying Fish Channel." At ebb tide, the channel's mud banks were out of the water as far as two miles off from the shore.

On the date set for the assault, the morning high tide would be at 6:59. Two hours later, the assault craft would be wallowing on the mud banks and would stay there—literally sitting ducks for shore batteries or bombing aircraft—until the next high tide at 7:19 P.M. Therefore, the landing forces would have only two hours to neutralize the fortifications on Wolmi-do, the island which commands the harbor, and to establish a beachhead in the downtown streets of Inchon, where the city reached the harbor. Concluding the Navy's presentation, Admiral Sherman said:

"If every possible geographical and naval handicap were listed—Inchon has 'em all."

The Army followed the Navy. General Collins felt the landing was too far in the rear and that the forces were inadequate. He feared that the enemy might have overwhelming troops in the city.

MacArthur listened quietly but unworriedly. When the others had finished, he arose and began speaking in a conversational tone.

He felt sure, he said, that many of the arguments presented against the landing would serve equally well for it. If the operation was that difficult, certainly the North Koreans would not be expecting it. While he felt the obstacles were great, they were not insurmountable. Smiling at Sherman, an old friend, he said that perhaps he had more confidence in the Navy than the Navy had in itself.

He accented the element of surprise. He recalled Wolfe's capture of Quebec two centuries before, when the defending Montcalm was sure no one could scale the river banks south of the city. Wolfe did, won a stunning victory—and the war. MacArthur emphasized the effect the landing at Inchon would have: cutting the enemy's supply lines, isolating him in the southern part of the Korean peninsula, squeezing him between the Inchon forces and General Walker's Eighth Army.

"The only alternative," he finished, "would be the continuation of the savage sacrifice we are making at Pusan, with no hope of relief in sight. Are you content to let our troops stay in the bloody perimeter like beef cattle in a slaughterhouse? Who would take the responsibility for such a tragedy? Certainly I will not."

When he had completed his case and sat down, Admiral Sherman whispered audibly: "A great voice in a great cause."

The Washington delegation returned home . . . and on August 29 MacArthur was authorized to proceed with the Inchon landing. He had, in fact, already proceeded, in order not to miss the September 15 deadline set by the Inchon tides.

Watching from his flagship, the *Mount McKinley*, MacArthur saw the first wave of marines go in with the high tide. They secured a beachhead without a fatality. The guns on Wolmi-do were silenced. Believing it too difficult for assault, the enemy had left Inchon lightly defended, as MacArthur had suspected. It fell—and Seoul was captured soon after that.

Then, caught in a giant pincers movement, with one jaw the X corps which had landed at Inchon and the other the Eighth Army in the south, the North Koreans literally came apart. Their supplies and reinforcements cut off, whole divisions retreated in disorder and ceased to function as organized units. In one month, one hundred and thirty thousand prisoners were taken. The landing at Inchon and the campaign which followed saved the Eighth Army from defeat—and probably saved the South Korean nation. The messages of congratulation which poured into MacArthur's headquarters included one from President Truman.

In a moving ceremony, MacArthur restored Syngman Rhee to his capital at Seoul and to the presidency of South Korea. Then, with the approval of the United Nations and the Joint Chiefs, he began his drive across the 38th parallel.

During the next few weeks, the United Nations forces, which were largely American but also included units from most of the free western nations of the world, moved straight for the Yalu River, which divided North Korea from Chinese Manchuria. Pyongyang, the North Korean capital, fell. On November 6, 1950, MacArthur issued a communiqué which said, in part:

The Korean war was brought to a practical end with the closing of the trap on enemy elements north of Pyongyang and seizure of the east coastal area, resulting in raising the number of enemy prisoners-of-war in our hands to well over 135,000 which, with other losses mounting to over 200,000, brought enemy casualties to 335,000, representing a fair estimate of North Korean total military strength. The defeat of the North Koreans and the destruction of their armies was thereby decisive.

It was indeed a decisive victory. But just twenty days later, on November 26, a whole new war started. The Red Chinese attacked from Manchuria in massive strength.

Throughout his battles against the North Koreans, MacArthur had been forbidden to bomb the bridges across the Yalu, to pursue enemy aircraft across the Yalu and even to bomb or otherwise destroy hydro-electric plants and supply dumps on the North Korean banks of the Yalu. The reasons were political and the right or wrong of them is still being debated in thousands of words in military and political papers.

Whether the orders were justified or not, the result was strangulating as far as the war against North Korea was concerned. Supplies moved freely across the bridges from Manchuria. Hostile aircraft, frequently manned by Russian pilots, were able to raid South Korea and then dart back across the Yalu to a happy sanctuary.

If the order was thwarting in the campaigns against the North Koreans, it was disastrous when the Red Chinese moved. His pleas to bomb the Yalu bridges denied, MacArthur and his forces watched in impotent frustration and despair as two complete Chinese field armies, nearing six hundred thousand men, poured across the Yalu bridges and attacked in overwhelming force.

Said MacArthur, "For the first time in military history a commander has been denied the use of his military power to safeguard the lives of his soldiers and the safety of his army."

In the fighting which followed, the United Nations forces were driven back. An element of one hundred and five thousand men was pinned against the sea on the east coast—and saved, with all their supplies and thousands of refugees, by a daring evacuation from Hungnam, which was "an Inchon in reverse."

General Walker was killed (in a jeep accident) and replaced by Lieutenant General Matthew Ridgway. The United Nations forces fell back across the 38th parallel under a massive Red Chinese offensive, which started on New Year's Eve, and the ensuing battle raged for days. Seoul was captured and by January 7 the Eighth Army, fighting valiantly, had been forced some seventy miles back of the 38th parallel.

On January 9, MacArthur flew to Korea for a conference with Ridgway. The result was a counterattack which carried the United Nations forces across the Han River, recaptured Inchon and Seoul and, by mid-April, had moved again to the 38th parallel.

There, where it had all started less than a year before, the forward line was re-established. Truce negotiations began on July 10, 1951, and an armistice resulted two years later, on July 27, 1953.

MacArthur was present for neither the truce nor the armistice. On April 11, 1951, President Truman relieved him of all duties in Korea and Japan, and ordered him home.

The reasons were political rather than military and these, like many other facets of the Korean War, must bear the judgment of history. It is sufficient here to note that there were strong differences of opinion between many of President Truman's advisors (and possibly the President himself) in Washington and MacArthur in Tokyo, as to the conduct of America's foreign policy in the Far East.

One incident leading up to the General's dismissal dealt with the delicate subject of Formosa. It was probably the greatest rift between MacArthur and the Truman administration. Asked by the Veterans of Foreign Wars to send a message to be read at a forthcoming annual encampment, and regarding the request as routine, MacArthur prepared such a message and sent it through Department of Army channels. A week later, he received a wire ordering him, in the President's name, to withdraw the statement. He tried but it was too late. His message had already been printed in the program and went out.

MacArthur's subject had been the island of Formosa, occupied then as now by the Nationalist Chinese, after their retirement from the mainland. MacArthur considered, and so stated, that the Nationalist Chinese were on Formosa legally, by Allied agreement. Truman, with his own reasons, considered the position of Formosa—and the Nationalist Chinese occupation there—as unfixed.

Complicating the Formosa matter was MacArthur's long argument with the Joint Chiefs of Staff regarding the right to defend the island, which he considered to be part of the defense of Japan—and Korea. He also felt that had Chiang Kai-shek been permitted to engage the Red Chinese on the mainland, they would have been too busy to enter the war in Korea. (He had created a small storm in Washington earlier when he had visited Chiang for one day.)

MacArthur had received a letter from Representative Joseph Martin of Massachusetts, Republican Minority Leader in the House, asking his views on a constituent's letter—which advocated the establishment of a second Asiatic front by Chiang Kai-shek. On March 20, MacArthur replied, in part:

My views and recommendations with respect to the situation created by Red China's entry into war against us in Korea have been submitted to Washington in most complete detail. Generally these views are well known and clearly understood, as they follow the pattern of meeting force with maximum counterforce as we have never failed to do in the past. Your view with respect to the utilization of the Chinese forces in Formosa is in conflict with neither logic nor this tradition.

On that same date, the Joint Chiefs radioed MacArthur, informing him of an impending peace move to be made by President Truman, who felt that efforts should be made through diplomatic channels to effect some kind of truce before another military move was made across the 38th parallel. Truman's thoughts were circulated to the United Nations.

Four days later, without consulting Washington or the United Nations, MacArthur made his own peace announcement. He was prepared to confer with the Red Chinese Commander in Korea for immediate surrender negotiations. He flew to Korea to be ready in case his proposal was accepted. (The text of it had been dropped by the thousands in Red Chinese Army positions as a psychological warfare gesture.)

To compound matters, Congressman Martin chose this time to release MacArthur's letter.

The General's peace proposal had been promptly repudiated by a startled and angry official Washington. Now, his views on Chiang's military activities, and their political potential, vis-à-vis the delicate balance between the Western and the Communist worlds, brought the wrath of the press down upon him—both European and American.

President Truman reacted characteristically and immediately. In his eyes, MacArthur had stepped too far over the fine dividing line which separates the military commander and the political leader. His message relieving MacArthur of all commands was curt and harsh. MacArthur read it without visible emotion.

"Jeanie," he told his wife, "we're going home."

17

☆ ☆ ☆ ☆ ☆

GENERAL Douglas MacArthur arrived in Japan as a conqueror. He left as a hero to the Japanese people.

The country's leading newspapers wrote of their faith and trust in him—and of their shock at his recall. The Emperor, against all protocol, requested an audience and bade the General an emotional farewell. The people of Yokohama commissioned a leading sculptor to create a bronze bust of him. On its base were inscribed the words: "General Douglas MacArthur, Liberator of Japan."

The three major political parties of the Diet sponsored a resolution of tribute, expressing the thanks of the nation. On the morning of his departure, at dawn, a crowd estimated at a million people lined the road from the Embassy to Haneda Airport, waving Japanese and American flags. Thousands more were at the airport itself, to cry the traditional farewell of the nation—"*Sayonara*."

The orders dismissing MacArthur from the service of his country after fifty-two years in uniform were received on April 11, 1951. On April 16, he was flying homeward. The "SCAP" insignia of the Supreme Commander on his C-54 had been painted over and, once again, it was the *Bataan*. Ac-

companying him, of course, were his wife and son. The senior
MacArthurs had not seen their native land for fourteen years.
Arthur had never seen it. As the *Bataan* flew past snow-
covered Mount Fuji, MacArthur said, "It will be a long time
before we see her again."

The wire MacArthur had received recalling him had included the words:

"You are authorized to have issued such orders as are
necessary to complete desired travel to such places as you
may select." They were as coldly impersonal as any other
military orders. They did not suggest that he drop by the
White House or the Pentagon for a cup of coffee, let alone
a hero's welcome. They seemed, instead, to suggest that he
travel to the oblivion of his choice.

Things didn't work out quite that way. The *Bataan* approached San Francisco after nightfall and, watching the
panorama of lights appear under the wing, MacArthur put
his arm around the shoulders of thirteen-year-old Arthur and
said, "We are home at last."

He had expected, he said later, to slip quietly into a hotel,
where he could polish up the address he had been invited
to give to the combined Houses of Congress. But, when the
Bataan taxied to a stop, the plane door opened on a surging
sea of Californians who had their own feelings as to the kind
of welcome he deserved. Governor Warren and Mayor Robinson of San Francisco led, you might say, the cheering section
through which MacArthur and his party finally made their
way to the hotel.

Whether to his surprise or not, Douglas MacArthur found
himself asked repeatedly if he intended to run for President.
The next morning, in an official ceremony at City Hall, he
made what sounded like a clear negative reply, although

there were many then and later who thought he could be persuaded to change his mind. He said:

"I was just asked if I intended to enter politics. My reply was no. I have no political aspirations whatsoever. I do not intend to run for political office, and I hope that my name will never be used in a political way. The only politics I have is contained in a single phrase known well to all of you—God Bless America."

His arrival in Washington was also in darkness and there again he faced a cheering throng of thousands who had waited patiently for his arrival at the airport. Rather ironically, the same Joint Chiefs of Staff who had at least *agreed* to his dismissal formed the official welcoming delegation—Generals Bradley, Collins and Vandenberg, and Admiral Sherman. With them was General Marshall, then Secretary of Defense.

The next day Douglas MacArthur delivered his greatest speech in a career which had coined many much-quoted phrases. Addressing the Senate and House, sitting in joint session, he began:

"I trust that you will do me the justice of receiving that which I have to say as solely expressing the considered viewpoint of a fellow American. I address you with neither rancor nor bitterness in the fading twilight of life with but one purpose in mind, to serve my country."

Rather than review his own career, as he might have done, MacArthur dwelt largely on the Asian scene he had just quitted. He pictured the changes the previous few years had brought to the Far East, its enlightenment, its new moral forces, its new outlook. He carefully expounded his attitude on the war in Korea, the strategic importance of Formosa; he paid tribute, of course, to his old friends, the Filipinos. Citing past decisions in the light of present dangers, he warned of the folly of appeasement. He had occasion to use a favorite phrase: "In war, there is no substitute for victory."

His concluding words, which brought the audience to its feet in a standing ovation of sincere applause, have been much quoted and doubtless will be long remembered:

"I have just left your sons fighting in Korea. They have met all tests there and I can report to you without reservations, they are splendid in every way.

"It was my constant effort to preserve them and end this savage conflict honorably and with the least loss of time and a minimum sacrifice of life. Its growing bloodshed has caused me the deepest anguish and anxiety. Those gallant men will remain often in my thoughts and in my prayers always.

"I am closing my fifty-two years of military service. When I joined the Army, even before the turn of the century, it was the fulfillment of all my boyish hopes and dreams.

"The world has turned over many times since I took the oath on the plain at West Point, and the hopes and dreams have long since vanished, but I still remember the refrain of one of the most popular barracks ballads of that day, which proclaimed, most proudly, that 'Old soldiers never die. They just fade away.'

"And like the old soldier of that ballad, I now close my military career and just fade away—an old soldier who tried to do his duty as God gave him the light to see that duty.

"Good-by."

18

★ ☆ ☆ ★ ☆

I T WOULD hardly be accurate to say that Douglas MacArthur actually "faded away" nor would it have been in character. New York gave him an almost hysterical ticker-tape parade. He made headlines and won admirers with his long and detailed testimony before a Congressional Committee investigating the conduct of the war in Korea.

He went on a speaking tour, which was carefully non-political, of eleven states crusading to—in his own words—revitalize the nation and save the freedom of representative government in America.

He declined to campaign for the Republican nomination as President in 1952, although he most certainly would have accepted it proudly had it been freely offered. He did agree, according to his intimates, to accept the Vice Presidential post should Senator Taft be nominated. He made the keynote address of the 1952 Republican Convention and then watched with profound disappointment while his old aide, General Dwight Eisenhower, ran away with the balloting.

In the meantime, Douglas MacArthur and his family had moved into a floor-large suite at the Waldorf Towers, in New York City. He accepted a long-standing offer to become

Chairman of the Board of the Remington Rand Corporation, an organization whose programs and policies he admired greatly. When it was merged with the Sperry Corporation, he was then elected Chairman of the Board of the new company, Sperry Rand.

The death of Douglas MacArthur, on April 5, 1964, was the occasion for national mourning and signaled a cross-country funeral ceremony which began in New York, continued to Washington, where the body lay in state at the Capitol rotunda, and then ended in Norfolk, Virginia. He was buried there in the MacArthur Memorial Museum, maintained by the state.

The legend of Douglas MacArthur was already well established before his death. It will continue to grow because his life was rich in the things from which legends spring—courage, heroism, action, patriotism, drama. His fifty-two years of service, including the four as a cadet at West Point, where the legend started, encompassed a span from cavalry charge to atomic bomb.

Today, one may not say with absolute certainty that MacArthur was right in Korea, or that Truman was right in firing him. Or whether Chiang should have opened a second front in Red China. It is possible, however, to leave this to the historians. Other facets of the MacArthur story are open for all to see.

As a general and a military leader his contemporaries rank Douglas MacArthur among the greatest in American history. The admission of some may be grudging, but it is there. Even if it were not, his personal achievements with the Rainbow Division in France, his defense of Bataan, his brilliantly executed war against the Japanese from Australia to the Philippines, his saving of Korea—all of these are real. His victories extend from St. Mihiel through Buna, Hollandia and Leyte to Inchon. His first star as a Brigadier General, in recognition of great leadership qualities, came in 1918, when he was thirty-eight years old. He served on active duty as a general officer for more than thirty years, ending with the five stars of a General of the Army.

No officer or enlisted man in American military service has ever received anything approaching the number of awards for personal bravery accorded MacArthur. They start with the highest, the Medal of Honor, and include the Distinguished Service Cross, three times; the Silver Star, seven times; the Distinguished Service Medal of the Army, five times; the Distinguished Service Medal of the Navy; the Distinguished Flying Cross; the Air Medal; the Bronze Star; the Purple Heart, twice; the Distinguished Unit Citation, four times; the Campaign Star, fifteen times; the Philippine Medal of Valor and some thirty other foreign decorations, including British Knighthood.

The stories of MacArthur's bravery, his disregard of danger and his seemingly well-founded belief that he bore a charmed life are endless, most of them recounted by companions at the scene who had heartily wished—at the time—that they weren't around. He had a firm belief—and demonstrated it— that "the old man" must show the men of his command "he can take it."

The breadth and depth of MacArthur's knowledge never failed to amaze his associates. He was born with brains, someone said, and spent a lifetime developing them. He was trained at West Point as an engineer (as well as a soldier). But in other fields—law, medicine, chemistry, philosophy and certainly history—he had a far better than average knowledge. His feats of memory were prodigious. For three days, with no memoranda or supporting documents, he answered Congressional Committee questions which covered intricate points of Asian history, some fine details of American foreign policy, the strength of the military power of several nations— all lucidly and without hesitation. Committee members were impressed, and said so.

At the memorable conference at Pearl Harbor in 1944, when he convinced President Roosevelt to accept his plan for processing the war in the Pacific, MacArthur talked for three hours without pausing to search for a word or a figure.

At the end, Roosevelt said, "Douglas, you've taught me more about the Pacific than I had known in all my previous life."

The very feat of getting Roosevelt to listen for three hours speaks volumes. As President, he was not a notable listener.

The men around MacArthur idolized him, and they document their devotion with stories of his deeds which exemplify everything that is best in human conduct, along with omnipotent wisdom. Others, from other points of vantage and view, have other opinions. Almost none of them debate such traits as ability, loyalty and courage, even though they may have questions about the omnipotent wisdom in certain areas.

The historians may have trouble in rendering final judgment, but one thing is certain—history will never ignore Douglas MacArthur.

BIBLIOGRAPHY

The following books are recommended for further reading on the life of Douglas MacArthur. General Whitney's is notable for its first-hand accounts of the Pacific war campaigns, Clark Lee's for its more subjective presentation, and Kenney's for its refreshing frankness.

Whitney, Major General Courtney. *MacArthur, His Rendezvous with History.* New York. Alfred A. Knopf, 1956.

Lee, Clark (and Richard Henschel). *Douglas MacArthur.* New York. Henry Holt and Company, 1952.

Willoughby, Major General Charles A. and Chamberlain, John. *MacArthur 1941-1951.* New York. McGraw-Hill Book Company, Inc.

Kenney, General George C. *The MacArthur I Know.* New York. Duell, Sloan and Pearce, 1951.

Huff, Colonel Sid. *My Fifteen Years With General MacArthur.* New York. Paperback Library Inc. 1964.

Kelley, Frank and Ryan, Cornelius. *MacArthur, Man of Action.* Garden City, New York. Doubleday & Company, Inc., 1950.

Ganoe, William Addleman. *MacArthur Close-Up.* New York. Vantage Press, 1962.

Miller, Francis Trevelyan. *General Douglas MacArthur, Fighter For Freedom.* Philadelphia. The John C. Winston Company.

Gunther, John. *The Riddle of MacArthur.* New York. Harper and Brothers, 1950.

Pratt, John M. *Revitalizing A Nation.* Chicago. The Heritage Foundation, 1952.

Reilly, Brigadier General Henry J. *Americans All, The Rainbow at War.* Columbus, Ohio. The F. J. Heer Printing Co., Publishers, 1936.

MacArthur, General of the Army Douglas. *Reminiscences.* New York. McGraw-Hill Book Company, 1964.

INDEX

CLARKE NEWLON

Prior to World War II, Clarke Newlon was a newspaper writer and editor in Dallas, Chicago and Cleveland. His wartime service included Air Force assignments in England, France, Germany and Egypt.

When the Department of Defense was established in 1947, Newlon served there four years and then was assigned to the NATO headquarters in Paris and in Oslo, Norway. Returning to the United States in 1955, his last assignment was as Chief of the Information Division, Headquarters, USAF.

Colonel Newlon left the Air Force in 1958 to become the editor of a technical space magazine. He moved from this position in 1961 to establish a writing corporation whose clients included the National Space and Aeronautics Administration, the U. S. Information Agency and industrial corporations.

Clarke Newlon lives in Washington, D. C., with his wife. Their two sons are in college. He is a member of the National Press Club, the International Club and the National Aviation Club.